Models for Teaching Writing-Craft Target Skills

MARCIA S. FREEMAN

with

LUANA K. MITTEN and RACHEL M. CHAPPELL

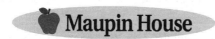
Maupin House

Models for Teaching Writing-Craft Target Skills

By Marcia S. Freeman with Luana K. Mitten and Rachel M. Chappell
©2005 Marcia Freeman
All Rights Reserved

Cover Design & Page Layout.....Hank McAfee

Library of Congress Cataloging-in-Publication Data

Freeman, Marcia S. (Marcia Sheehan), 1937-
  Models for teaching writing-craft target skills / by Marcia S. Freeman
with Rachel M. Chappell and Luana K. Mitten.
     p. cm.
  Includes index.
  ISBN 0-929895-80-0
  1. English language--Composition and exercises--Study and teaching. 2.
Children--Books and reading. 3. Children's literature--Bibliography. I.
Chappell, Rachel M., 1978- II. Mitten, Luana K. III. Title.
  LB1576.F7294 2005
  372.62'3--dc22

                                    2005006140

ISBN-10: 0-929895-80-0
ISBN-13: 978-0-929895-80-2

10 9 8 7 6 5 4 3 2

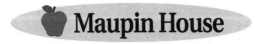

Maupin House Publishing, Inc.
PO Box 90148 • Gainesville, FL 32607
1-800-524-0634 • 352-373-5588 • 352-373-5546 (fax)

www.maupinhouse.com • email: info@maupinhouse.com

Publishing Professional Resources that Improve Classroom Performance

Contents

■ ■

Acknowledgements

This book would not have been possible without the help of a number of dedicated educators. I am especially grateful to Luana K. Mitten and Rachel Chappell, whose comments and counsel during the planning and drafting of the manuscript, as well as their input into the bibliographies, was invaluable.

I also want to thank the following teachers and librarians from schools implementing CraftPlus™, who contributed lists of their favorite books and identified the writing craft the authors used.

Mary Beth Laiti (Florida)
Debbie Vogel and the teachers at Douglas Road Elementary (Michigan)
Bo Bush, librarian (Louisiana)
Michelle Hostetler (Ohio)
Marilyn Cafaro (Florida)

As always, thanks to Mike Freeman, editor extraordinaire.

Marcia S. Freeman
April 2005

Chapter One

INTRODUCTION TO TEACHING TARGET SKILLS WITH MODELS

Writing craft is the wonderful set of skills and techniques that writers know and use to make their writing clear and interesting. Therefore, craft instruction is a critical component of effective writing education. That instruction, provided in a classroom writing-workshop environment, is the key to writing competency. The writing workshop provides the setting and conditions for students to learn and practice writing craft and use the writing process (prewriting, composing, getting a response, revising, and editing). Writing-craft lessons provide the tools students need to effectively organize, compose, and revise. Remember, *"Writing process is what writers do; writing craft is what they know."*

In *The Rise and Fall of English*, Robert Scholes, Andrew W. Mellon Professor of Humanities at Brown University, advises, *"Our range, our capabilities go no further than craft. Even in creative writing courses, craft is all that can be taught."* He also tells us, *"Our aim should be to help students learn how to produce a good, workmanlike job with a written piece whenever they need to. It means mastering the medium through the study of models."*

The Purpose of This Book

I have compiled the bibliographies of this book for the growing number of teachers who, like you, have recognized the validity of Professor Scholes' observation and are centering their writing instruction on writing craft. A vital part of your instruction is showing students how other authors have applied the craft skills you are teaching. I have arranged these bibliographies by specific skill and genre. They will provide you with a solid starting set of strong models for your instruction.

The bibliographies include both Newbery and Caldecott award winners. Classics and new books, by both known authors and new authors, are also listed. Most of the books are children's picture books, which are particularly engaging to young readers. Some of the lists are extensive and some are not. Bibliographies, such as these, are a perpetual work in progress. You and your students will want to add to them as you find other books that also effectively model particular writing-craft skills.

Writing Craft and the Reading Connection

Reading researcher T. Shanahan (1997) notes that *"Awareness of an author's choices is central to effective critical reading, but this information is well hidden in text, and children become aware of it rather late in their development. Writing, because it affords one an insider's view of this aspect of text, provides a powerful, complementary way of thinking about reading that would not be available if reading and writing were identical."*

Students can only recognize the choices authors make if they are making these very same ones themselves. A major area of author choice is writing craft. I have found that whe[n] ... ing this craft starting in kinderga... until *"rather late in their de...*

When s... to recognize the craf... they have internali... od sign when students... e reading. Not all published... tudents trained to look for... with great glee that a seco... eeman, this book has n...

Handwritten note:

→ Target Skill — using strong verbs

Readers need to visualize
writers need to create
imagery

→ Give the author a thumbs up each time you emphasize a verb with your voice (encourage oooh...)

* words help you visualize

Margin note: * strong verbs

Teaching

The following ... ng-craft lesson using a ... that is the objective of a writing-craft l... get Skill™. (I have chosen an important craft skill, *strong-verb writing*, to illustrate the process).

1. **Introduce the Target Skill and present a literature model:**
    (For my example) Tell your students that because readers need to visualize, writers must create imagery and that one way to do that is by using strong verbs. Point out the strong-verb writing in the literature model you have selected. During the reading demonstration, invite students to give the author a thumbs-up each time you emphasize a verb with your voice. *"The cow is (licking) her calf."* Coach them how to respond with a thumbs-up and even to simultaneously say, *"Oooooh, **licking**!"*

2. **Discuss the technique:**
    Ask your students: *Can you visualize what is happening if I do not show you the pictures? Which is more helpful? The cow is with her calf, or the cow is licking her calf?*

3. **Model the technique orally,** using and talking about a photo. Model two-three sentences.
    In my photo, a horse is (nibbling) an apple. Invite your students to

respond to the verb **nibbling** with a thumbs-up and an *"Oooh, nibbling!"* Continue with two more sentences about the horse and what it is doing. *The horse's mane is **hanging** do~~wn his~~ ~~~~* up. *"Oooh, **hanging**!"*

4. **Students, in partnerships** ~~o~~ **orally.** They each talk abou~~t~~ Photographs are an excellen~~t~~ select pictures that match th~~e~~ plenty to say about it. They w~~ill~~ pertinent to the subject of th~~e~~

✳ Guide them through the art~~~~ person, animal, or object do~~~~ up and *"Oooh"* responses for~~~~

5. **Students try the technique o**~~f~~ sentences about their photo. depends on their vocabularie~~s~~ vocabulary training, reading the level, each student can hit

[handwritten note:] Use photographs / Horse **nibbling** an apple / Guide students through / person || animal || object

6. **You and peers respond to student writing**: Students **say** or **read** their sentences to another student. The listener compliments the writer's use of the Target Skill (craft technique) with a sticker or a color mark.

(After the lesson)

7. **Students practice the Target Skill** in their independent writing, such as in literacy centers, science journals, literature response pieces, and in personal journals. Practicing writing-craft skills in different venues encourages students to take risks and play with writing craft. It is through this kind of practice that students become creative and competent writers.

8. **Students apply the Target Skill(s) in an assessed piece**. Once students have had ample opportunity to practice a target skill or skills, you will want to see if they can apply the skills to a prompted *[handwritten: pictures ❯]* (photo or verbal) piece. They might take the piece through the entire writing process (pre-write, compose, peer conference, revise, and edit) or write in a draft in a timed session.

    The rubric criterion for this assessed piece is the application of one or more of the specific, pre-identified Target Skills. Note how this gives every student an opportunity to succeed.

Writing-Craft Instruction Resources

Although I have addressed in this book the most important writing-craft techniques for elementary and middle-school student writers, there are other appropriate techniques for these writers. You will find much more information about writing craft and how to teach it in my books, *Building a Writing Community* and *Teaching the Youngest Writers*. For annotated samples of a variety of expository writing models, refer to my book, *Listen to This: Developing an Ear for Expository*. Also, see ADDITIONAL RESOURCES in the back of this book for a more extensive bibliography of professional books and information about writing instruction.

If you and your colleagues are implementing *CraftPlus™*, my writing program and staff development resource, you will find that this book identifies the models you need for teaching many of the writing-craft Target Skills detailed in the program's curriculum.

Using Literature Models

As you use literature models when teaching writing-craft skills, you should bear in mind the following principles:

- Books have two elements: content and craft. Always read a book to students for its content before analyzing it for the writing craft the author demonstrates. During your initial reading, children will want to, and should, focus on content. During a subsequent reading session, in which you invite open discussion of the book as you and your students explore it, draw their attention to the writing craft you next intend to teach.

- Always read literature that is well-written (employs rich vocabulary and active verbs; is organized, engaging, imaginative, accurate, pleasant-sounding, and well-illustrated). That is, literature filled with the writing craft identified in this book.

- Look for writing craft in all the books and magazines you regularly use throughout your instructional days. The learning potential for children from familiar text is great.

- Use literature your students have heard or read themselves. Use literature from assorted genres to develop your students' ears for the different genres. For instance, students who hear lots of informational text learn that its authors usually proceed from the general to the specific. The writer tells what a whale looks like before he gets into the details about how it breathes.

- In intermediate grades and higher, use children's picture books freely. These students will appreciate the format, and because they can easily understand its content, they are able to concentrate on its writing craft.

- ELL students and students with learning difficulties also benefit from the use of children's picture books. Identifying and discussing writing craft in high-interest texts (regardless of reading level) supports their own practice of writing craft.

Note: Writing craft is the same for writers of all ages. For example, writers from six to ninety-six need to use strong verbs to help their readers visualize. Age-related differences show up in the sophistication level of the skill application, which reflects the level of the writer's vocabulary and life experiences.

> Student writing can be another, powerful source of models for teaching writing-craft skills. Students need to see how other young writers apply the craft. They say to themselves, "I can do that, too!"

General Writing Skills and Genre-Associated Skills

This book has two parts. In Chapter 2, I list literature models for general writing-craft Target Skills that are applicable to all genres. In Chapter 3, I describe the characteristics of individual genres and I list literature models for each. In addition, models for Target Skills that are specific to a given genre are provided.

In both Chapters 2 and 3, I illustrate some of the craft skills with examples from professional books and student writing. These examples should help you and your students find additional models from your favorite books in your school library and classroom.

> Helpful hint: Gather your grade team or colleagues to group-browse through your school library for models of the genres and writing craft in this book.

Definition of Terms

Trade books are both hardcover and paperback books that are, or were originally, published by general children's publishers, such as HarperCollins, Putnam, Dell, Puffin, Candlewick, Northland, Rourke, etc. They may be **fiction**, **non-fiction concept books**, **personal** and **informational narratives**, or **informational expository** texts. They may be art- or photo-illustrated. They are the kind of books you will find in your school or public library, and purchased at bookstores or online.

Educational publications are books produced by educational publishers, such as Rourke, Newbridge, Rand McNally, Children's Press, Scholastic, The Wright Group, Dominie Press, Benchmark, etc. These books are generally available from catalogs. They are usually paperbacks, and some are available in a Big Book format and student classroom sets. Many are leveled and come from guided-reading series. They also may be **fiction**, **non-fiction concept books**, **personal** and informational narratives, or informational expository texts.

(See ADDITIONAL RESOURCES in the back of this book for information about the educational publishers whose books appear as models).

Using the Lists

- A series of boxes *before* each listed title allows you to indicate where you can find the book at your school: **L** Library, **CR** Classroom, **BR** Book Room, **P** Personal Collection. You might want to add (H) to indicate if is located at your home.

- Space *after* each list allows you and your students to add favorite books that can serve also as models of genre-specific or general writing-craft skills.

- For simplicity's sake, just the title and author of trade books are listed. You can find these books by either of these two attributes when searching library catalogs and Internet sources.

- Encourage your media specialist to purchase the books you identify that are rich in the writing craft you are teaching.

- Books available from educational publishers include title, author, publisher, and series title where appropriate.

- Books specifically suited for fifth through eighth grades are indicated by (**intermediate**).

- Many authors are notable for their use of writing craft. If the book listed for a particular author is not available, look for another book by the same author. Chances are, it will demonstrate the same writing craft.

(**Reminder:** The books listed in the categories of trade and educational publications may be fiction or non-fiction. *Literature* encompasses both fiction and non-fiction).

Chapter Two

GENERAL WRITING-CRAFT SKILLS

■ ▪

Most writing-craft skills can be applied across all genres. These skills include: description using strong verbs and an adjectival vocabulary of attributes; literary devices; specificity; alliteration; contrast; embedded definitions; clues to provide for reader inference; repetition; beginning and ending techniques; supporting details; organization schema, including text structures; sentence variation; and voice techniques. Some of these general craft skills may have specific variations that apply to their use in a particular genre.

This chapter briefly discusses each of the major, general writing craft-skills, provides one or two text examples that illustrate the skill, and then lists books—across many genres—that you can use for strong models of the particular skill. The next chapter discusses any genre-specific variations of the general skills.

Description: Skills for Creating Imagery

One of the primary tasks for writers in all genres is to help their readers **visualize**. To do this, both expository and narrative writers create imagery through a number of writing-craft techniques that I group under the general term **description**. Here are some of the most common ones:

· strong verbs

· adjectives associated with a large variety of attributes (color, texture, function, etc.)

· comparisons, such as similes, metaphors, and others

· personification

· onomatopoeia

· specificity

> Dialogue tags contribute to imagery as well. But since they are specific to narrative genres, you will find the models for this craft skill in Chapter 3.

Student writers need facility with description. Particularly in expository writing, descriptive details provide a great deal of the requisite elaboration. Most state student-writing-assessment rubrics include a factor for elaboration. The rubric may refer to it as "elaboration" or as "development of ideas."

Description is an important component of all genres. The following books have a strong descriptive component and can serve as excellent overall models of the various craft-skills that make up descriptive writing. (See also books listed under each of the other specific skills for creating imagery: strong verbs, attribute adjectives, comparisons, onomatopoeia, specificity, and personification).

Books Rich in Description

L	CR	BR	P	TRADE BOOK MODELS
				Animals and Their Colors, Stephanie Maze
				Canoe Days, Gary Paulsen
				If Only I Could Fly, Brod Bagert
				It's Winter, Linda Glaser
				Let Me Be The Boss, Brod Bagert
				Like a Windy Day, Frank and Devin Asch
				Little Green, Keith Baker
				Marsh Morning, Marianne Berkes
				Rabbits and Raindrops, Jim Arnosky
				Roxaboxen, Alice McLerran
				Twilight Comes Twice, Ralph Fletcher
				Verses for Dad's Heart, Steven Layne
				Where the Sidewalk Ends, Shel Silverstein **(intermediate)**
				White Snow, Bright Snow, Alvin Tresselt

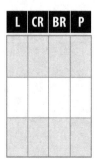

L	CR	BR	P	EDUCATIONAL BOOK MODELS
				A Rain Forest Adventure, Christine and Anton Economos (Newbridge, *Discovery Links*)
				Animals in Hiding, Melvin Berger (Newbridge, *Early Science*), Big Book
				As Big As a Whale, Melvin Berger (Newbridge, *Early Science*), Big Book

L	CR	BR	P	EDUCATIONAL BOOK MODELS (cont.)
				Dirt, Luana K. Mitten and Mary Wagner (Rourke, *Readers for Writers*)
				Everything Under the Sun, Marcia S. Freeman (Rourke, *Readers for Writers*), Big Book
				Insects, Marcia S. Freeman (Rourke, *Readers for Writers*)
				It's Best to Leave a Snake Alone, Allan Fowler (Children's Press), Big Book
				Living Colors, Marcia S. Freeman (Rourke, *Readers for Writers*)
				Our Attribute Walk, Luana K. Mitten and Mary Wagner (Rourke, *Readers for Writers*)
				Properties of Materials, Marcia S. Freeman (Newbridge, *Early Science*), Big Book
				Shorebirds, Melissa Stewart (Newbridge, *Ranger Rick*), Big Book
				The Web of Life, Melvin Berger (Newbridge, *Ranger Rick*), Big Book
				Wetlands, Marcia S. Freeman (Newbridge, *Early Science*), Big Book
				What Plant Is This?, Marcia S. Freeman (Rourke, *Readers for Writers*), Big Book
				Woolly Sheep and Hungry Goats, Allan Fowler (Children's Press), Big Book
				Why Polar Bears Like Snow…And Flamingos Don't, Nancy White (Benchmark, *Navigators*)
				_____
				_____
				_____
				_____
				_____

Strong Verbs

Good readers visualize. Good writers help them do that by creating imagery. **Strong-verb** writing is one of a writer's most powerful imagery tools and, as such, is the most important early Target Skill craft lesson for all writers. I recommend that it be your first writing-craft lesson.

*The bird made not a sound as we **followed** our wagon tracks home. He **pecked** at some seeds when we **stopped** and ate our supper of cold beans and cornbread. When night came, we **wrapped** a sack around the edge of the cage before we **snuggled** into our blankets.*

Fiction (*The Gift*, Marcia S. Freeman)

*Eagles **use** their claws, called talons, to **grab** their food. They **swoop** and **snatch** fish right out of the water…They can **pick up** animals **flapping** and **fighting** to get free.*

Informational text (*Getting Dinner*, Jennifer Blizin Gillis)

L	CR	BR	P	TRADE BOOK MODELS
				Boo to a Goose, Mem Fox
				Brave Irene, William Steig
				Bunny Bungalow, Cynthia Rylant
				Central Park Serenade, Laura Godwin
				Clap Your Hands, Lorinda Bryan Cauley
				Happy Birthday, Moon, Frank Asch
				It's Spring!, Samantha Berger and Pamela Chanko
				It's Winter, Linda Glaser
				Kite Sail High, Ruth Heller
				Like a Windy Day, Frank and Devin Asch
				Little Green, Keith Baker
				Mama Cat Has Three Kittens, Denise Fleming
				Mice Squeak, We Speak, Tomie dePaola
				Mike Fink, Steven Kellogg
				Morning, Noon, and Night, Jean Craighead George
				Old Black Fly, Jim Aylesworth
				Puffins Climb, Penguins Rhyme, Bruce McMillan
				Rabbits and Raindrops, Jim Arnosky
				Raccoons and Ripe Corn, Jim Arnosky
				Rainbow Fish, Marcus Pfister
				Stellaluna, Janell Cannon
				The Armadillo from Amarillo, Lynne Cherry
				The Cookie-Store Cat, Cynthia Rylant
				The Everglades, Jean Craighead George

L	CR	BR	P

TRADE BOOK MODELS (cont.)

The Gift, Marcia S. Freeman

The Relatives Came, Cynthia Rylant

The Slippery Slope, Lemony Snicket (**intermediate**)

The Very Clumsy Click Beetle, Eric Carle

The Very Quiet Cricket, Eric Carle

The Very Hungry Caterpillar, Eric Carle

Thunder Cake, Patricia Polacco

Town Mouse, Country Mouse, Jan Brett

Trucks, Trucks, Trucks, Peter Sis

Twilight Comes Twice, Ralph Fletcher

Verdi, Janell Cannon

When I Was Young in the Mountains, Cynthia Rylant

Where the Wild Things Are, Maurice Sendak

L	CR	BR	P

EDUCATIONAL BOOK MODELS

Animal Lives, Marcia S. Freeman (Rourke, *Readers for Writers*), Big Book

As Big As a Whale, Melvin Berger (Newbridge, *Ranger Rick*), Big Book

Bean, David M. Schwartz (CTP, *Life Cycles Science Series*)

Blood, Fay Robinson (The Wright Group, *TWIG Books*)

Getting Dinner, Jennifer Blizin Gillis (Rourke, *Readers for Writers*)

Giants, Wendy Blaxland (Scholastic, *Reading Discovery*)

Let's Look At Rocks, Luana K. Mitten and Mary Wagner (Rourke, *Readers for Writers*)

Mammal Moms, Marcia S. Freeman (Rourke, *Readers for Writers*)

Squirrels All Year Long, Melvin Berger (Newbridge, *Early Science*), Big Book

Spring, Tanya Thayer (Lerner Publishing, *First Step*)

Sticky Stuff, Luana K. Mitten and Mary Wagner (Rourke, *Readers for Writers*)

You Are a Scientist, Marcia S. Freeman (Rourke, *Readers for Writers*), Big Book

L	CR	BR	P

EDUCATIONAL BOOK MODELS (cont.)

_____

_____

_____

_____

_____

Attribute Adjectives

Adjectives, if used judiciously, help readers visualize, but an overabundance of them makes for silly writing. And no matter how many adjectives a writer uses, if the writing lacks strong verbs, it is weak writing. Contrast these examples:

Sleek squirrels scamper across the tree's rough bark. (Judicious use of adjectives and a strong verb).

The beady-eyed, whiskered, bushy-tailed, smooth and sleek gray squirrel is on the tree. (Too many adjectives and no active verb equals weak writing).

Adjectives can describe sensory attributes, such as color, texture, smell, taste, age, and size, with very specific vocabulary (purple, smooth, acrid, bitter, ten-year-old, fourteen-inch). Other adjectival vocabulary is non-specific (small, young) or comparative (as green as a lime, like licorice, satiny).

L	CR	BR	P	TRADE BOOK MODELS
				A Pinky is a Baby Mouse: And Other Baby Animal Names, Pam Muñoz Ryan
				Brave Irene, William Steig
				Bunny Cakes, Rosemary Wells
				Flower Garden, Eve Bunting
				Growing Colors, Bruce McMillan
				Hailstones and Halibut Bones, Mary O'Neill
				Have You Seen Trees?, Joanne Oppenheim
				Hey, Al, Arthur Yoriuk
				Jumanji, Chris Van Allsburg
				Kenya's Word, Linda Trice
				Mirandy and Brother Wind, Pat McKissack
				Miss Tizzy, Libba Moore Gray
				Nothing Ever Happens on 90th Street, Roni Schotter

L	CR	BR	P

TRADE BOOK MODELS (cont.)

Owl Moon, Jane Yolen

Polar Express, Chris Van Allsburg

Rainbow Fish, Marcus Pfister

Rainbows All Around Me, Sandra L. Pinkney

Shades of Black, Sandra L. Pinkney

Song and Dance Man, Karen Ackerman

So You Want to Be President?, Judith St. George (Caldecott Award)

"Slowly, Slowly, Slowly," said the Sloth, Eric Carle

Stellaluna, Janell Cannon

Tacky the Penguin, Helen Lester

The Important Book, Margaret Wise Brown ✳

The Winter Room, Gary Paulsen (**intermediate**)

Three Pebbles and a Song, Eileen Spinelli

Town Mouse, Country Mouse, Jan Brett

Trupp, Janell Cannon

White Snow, Bright Snow, Alvin Tresselt

Who am I?, Alain Crozon and Aurelie Lanchais

Verdi, Janell Cannon

L	CR	BR	P

EDUCATIONAL BOOK MODELS

Among the Flowers, David M. Schwartz (CTP, *Look Once, Look Again Science Series*)

As Big As a Whale, Melvin Berger (Newbridge, *Ranger Rick*), Big Book

Flavors From Plants, Jennifer Blizin Gillis (Rourke, *Readers for Writers*)

Listen to This, Patty Whitehouse (Rourke, *Readers for Writers*)

Living Colors, Marcia S. Freeman (Rourke, *Readers for Writers*)

Made of Metal, Patty Whitehouse (Rourke, *Readers for Writers*)

Our Attribute Walk, Luana K. Mitten and Mary Wagner (Rourke, *Readers for Writers*)

L	CR	BR	P	EDUCATIONAL BOOK MODELS (cont.)
				Properties of Materials, Marcia S. Freeman (Newbridge, *Early Science*), Big Book
				Put It Together, Patty Whitehouse (Rourke, *Readers for Writers*)
				The Web of Life, Melvin Berger (Newbridge, *Ranger Rick*), Big Book
				Spiders Are Special Animals, Fred and Jeanne Biddulph (Wright Group, *Sunshine Science Series*)
				Sunflower, David M. Schwartz (CTP, *Life Cycles Science Series*)
				What Plant is This?, Marcia S. Freeman (Rourke, *Readers for Writers*), Big Book
				Woolly Sheep and Hungry Goats, Allan Fowler (Children's Press), Big Book
				_____
				_____
				_____
				_____
				_____

Literary Devices for Comparison

Literary devices are composing skills that writers use to create imagery, make comparisons, provide a shortcut to comprehension, or produce a pleasing sound. They include such things as figurative language; comparisons (simile, metaphor, personification, analogy, and allusion); euphony (rhyme and alliteration); and onomatopoeia (imitating sounds with words). In this sub-section, we will look at composing skills for comparison.

Writers frequently use similes and metaphors to compare one thing to another based on a single common attribute. But they also effectively employ a number of other ways to make such comparisons.

1. Simile

A formal **simile** uses the format *as…as…* to compare two things in terms of one attribute. In a simile, the writer reveals the attribute.

Where is the animal <u>as clear as glass</u>?
  (*Animals in Hiding*, Melvin Berger)

L	CR	BR	P	TRADE BOOK MODELS
				A. Lincoln and Me, Louise Borden
				As: A Surfeit of Similes, Norton Juster
				I Love You the Purplest, Barbara Joosse
				Land of the Dark, Land of the Light: The Arctic National Wildlife Refuge, Karen Pandell
				More Similes, Joan Hanson
				One Small Place by the Sea, Barbara Brenner
				Punia and the King of Sharks, Lee Wardlaw
				Roll of Thunder, Hear My Cry, Mildred Taylor **(intermediate)**
				Sarah, Plain and Tall, Patricia MacLachlan
				Snakes Are Hunters, Patricia Lauber
				The Honey Makers, Gail Gibbons
				The Mitten, Jan Brett
				The Reptile Room, Lemony Snicket **(intermediate)**
				Where the Red Fern Grows, Wilson Rawls **(intermediate)**
				The Underwater Alphabet Book, Jerry Pallotta

L	CR	BR	P	EDUCATIONAL BOOK MODELS
				Animals in Hiding, Melvin Berger (Newbridge, *Early Science*), Big Book
				As Big As a Whale, Melvin Berger (Newbridge, *Ranger Rick*), Big Book
				Feeling Things, Allan Fowler (Children's Press), Big Book
				Frogs and Toads and Tadpoles, Too!, Allan Fowler (Children's Press), Big Book
				Is it Alive?, Marcia S. Freeman (Newbridge, *Early Science*), Big Book
				It Could Still Be a Fish, Allan Fowler (Children's Press), Big Book
				It Could Still Be a Tree, Allan Fowler (Children's Press), Big Book
				One Spring Day and Night, Patty Whitehouse (Rourke, *Readers for Writers*)

L	CR	BR	P	
				EDUCATIONAL BOOK MODELS (cont.)

Wetlands, Marcia S. Freeman (Newbridge, *Early Science*), Big Book

What Plant is This?, Marcia S. Freeman (Rourke, *Readers for Writers*), Big Book

You Are a Scientist, Marcia S. Freeman (Rourke, *Readers for Writers*), Big Book

_____

_____

_____

_____

_____

2. Metaphor

A **metaphor** highlights an attribute of something by calling it something else that is a prime example of that attribute. Thus, even though the writer does not explicitly identify this attribute, the reader is able to infer it. Some examples will clarify the concept: Call someone *an ox* and the reader will infer *strength;* Call someone *a shrimp* and the reader will infer *small*; *a weasel*: *sneaky and wily*; *a lion*: *brave*; and so on.

My breath was a fog in the frosty air.
   (*Night in the Barn*, Faye Gibbons)

The hurdler took off, a gazelle, popping over the hurdles without a falter.
   (high-school student example)

L	CR	BR	P	TRADE BOOK MODELS
				Canoe Days, Gary Paulsen
				From the Mixed-up Files of Mrs. Basil E. Frankweiler, E.L. Konigsburg (Newbery Award)
				In November, Cynthia Rylant
				Mud is Cake, Pam Muñoz Ryan
				Night in the Barn, Faye Gibbons
				Roll of Thunder, Hear My Cry, Mildred Taylor **(intermediate)**
				Shades of Black, Sandra L. Pinkney
				So You Want to Be President?, Judith St. George (Caldecott Award)

L	CR	BR	P

TRADE BOOK MODELS (cont.)

Swimmy, Leo Lionni

The Honey Makers, Gail Gibbons

The Slippery Slope, Lemony Snicket (**intermediate**)

Twilight Comes Twice, Ralph Fletcher

Where the Red Fern Grows, Wilson Rawls

L	CR	BR	P

EDUCATIONAL BOOK MODELS

It's a Good Thing There Are Insects, Allan Fowler (Children's Press), Big Book

Sea Anemones, Lynn M. Stone (Rourke, Science Under the Sea)

The American Flag, Lynda Sorensen (Rourke)

_____

_____

_____

_____

_____

3. Other ways to make comparisons

There is no rule that says writers must use only similes and metaphors to make **comparisons**. Writers use language in many other creative ways to get the job of describing by comparison done. For example, they use the comparative suffixes *-er* or *-est*, the word *like*, add the suffix *like* to a word (as in *ghostlike*), or use phrases such as: *…reminds(ed) me of…* and *so…that…*

*The elephant is **bigger** than the lion.*
    (student writer)

*…the Saguaro's red, **fig-like** fruit.*
    (*Life in the Desert*, Melvin Berger)

*The raccoon's fur was coarse **like** straw.*
    (student writer)

*The lake **reminds me of** the pond behind my uncle's house. They have the same pebbly edge.*
    (student writer)

*The dog is **so big that** his feet hung over the front seat when he rode in the car.*
(student writer)

Good readers visualize, and all these comparison techniques create imagery that helps them do that. Providing strong imagery is one of a writer's primary responsibilities to his readers.

L	CR	BR	P	TRADE BOOK MODELS
				Amos & Boris, William Steig
				Baby Whales Drink Milk, Barbara Juster Esbensen
				Canoe Days, Gary Paulsen
				Eloise, Kay Thompson
				Fireflies in the Night, Judy Hawes
				Germs Make Me Sick!, Melvin Berger
				Going West, Jean Van Leeuwen
				Hailstones and Halibut Bones, Mary O'Neill
				I Love You the Purplest, Barbara Joosse
				It's Winter, Glaser, Linda
				My Visit to the Aquarium, Aliki
				Pickles to Pittsburgh, Judi Barrett
				Sharks, Seymour Simon
				Snakes Are Hunters, Patricia Lauber
				So You Want to Be President?, Judith St. George (Caldecott Award)
				Tar Beach, Faith Ringgold
				The Armadillo from Amarillo, Lynne Cherry **(intermediate)**
				The Cloud Book, Tomie dePaola
				The Cookie-Store Cat, Cynthia Rylant
				The Gift, Marcia S. Freeman
				The Ticky-Tacky Doll, Cynthia Rylant
				The Underwater Alphabet Book, Jerry Pallotta
				Tico and the Golden Wings, Leo Lionni
				Two Bad Ants, Chris Van Allsburg
				Whales, Cynthia Rylant
				What Happens to a Hamburger?, Paul Showers

L	CR	BR	P

EDUCATIONAL BOOK MODELS

A Katydid's Life, Nic Bishop (The Wright Group, *TWIG Books)*

Animal Covers, Luana K. Mitten and Mary Wagner (Rourke, *Readers for Writers)*

Blood, Fay Robinson (The Wright Group, *TWIG Books)*

Getting Dinner, Jennifer Blizin Gillis (Rourke, *Readers for Writers)*

It Could Still Be a Fish, Allan Fowler (Children's Press), Big Book

It Could Still Be a Rock, Allan Fowler (Children's Press), Big Book

Life in the Desert, Melvin Berger (Newbridge, *Ranger Rick)*, Big Book

Reptiles, Lynn Stone (Rourke, *Animals in Disguise)*

Sea Anemones, Lynn M. Stone (Rourke, *Science Under the Sea)*

Sponges, Lynn M. Stone (Rourke, *Science Under the Sea)*

Sunflower, David M. Schwartz (CTP, *Life Cycles Science Series)*

The Web of Life, Melvin Berger (Newbridge, *Ranger Rick)*, Big Book

Refer to **Expository: Informational Text Structure - Comparison** in **Chapter Three** for comparison by multiple attributes.

Personification

Personification attributes people-like characteristics to inanimate objects. It is therefore a kind of metaphor.

*The **leaves danced** across the lawn while the trees flung their branches this way and that.*

L	CR	BR	P	TRADE BOOK MODELS
				Brave Irene, William Steig
				Chicka Chicka Boom Boom, Bill Martin Jr. and John Archambault
				Eaglet's World, Evelyn White Minshull
				In November, Cynthia Rylant
				It's Winter, Linda Glaser
				Like Butter on Pancakes, Jonathan London
				Manatee: On Location, Kathy Darling
				Mike Mulligan and His Steam Shovel, Virginia Lee Burton
				Paddle-to-the-Sea, Holling Clancy Holling
				Seal Pup Grows Up: The Story of a Harbor Seal, Kathleen Weidner Zoehfeld
				The Amazing Bone, William Steig
				The Gift, Marcia S. Freeman
				The Giving Tree, Shel Silverstein
				The Little Engine That Could, Watty Piper
				Whales, Cynthia Rylant

L	CR	BR	P	EDUCATIONAL BOOK MODELS
				Crocodile Tea, Marcia Vaughan (Rigby)
				The Three Little Pigs, Brenda Parkes (Rigby)
				The Runaway Pizza, Brenda Parkes (Rigby)
				Yum! Yuck!, Michaela Morgan (Rigby)
				_____
				_____
				_____
				_____
				_____
				_____

Onomatopoeia

Onomatopoeia is the use of words (which may be made-up words) that when spoken imitate a sound. This sound is related to the topic. Sounds play a part in imagery.

Writers use creative phonetic spelling to write some of the sounds. Author Peter Spier creates wonderful spellings for the sounds of such things as a flushing toilet, animal calls, and machinery.

*The drums sounded, **boom, boom, boom**, on the wrong beat. The band director yelled, "Noooooooooooooooooo!"*
   (*student writing*)

L	CR	BR	P	TRADE BOOK MODELS
				Brave Irene, William Steig
				Central Park Serenade, Laura Godwin
				Chicka Chicka Boom Boom, Bill Martin Jr. and John Archambault
				Click, Clack, Moo: Cows That Type, Doreen Cronin
				Cock-a-Doodle Doo!: What Does It Sound Like to You?, Marc Robinson
				Commotion in the Ocean, Giles Andreae
				Country Crossing, Jim Aylesworth
				Crash! Bang! Boom!, Peter Spier
				Crow Boy, Taro Yashima
				Crunch Munch, Jonathan London
				Froggy Gets Dressed, Jonathan London
				Froggy Goes to the Doctor, Jonathan London
				Froggy Learns to Swim, Jonathan London
				It's Winter, Linda Glaser
				Little Quack, Lauren Thompson
				Marsh Morning, Marianne Berkes
				Mice Squeak, We Speak, Tomie dePaola
				Mouse Mess, Linnea Riley
				Morning, Noon, and Night, Jean Craighead George
				Mr. Noisy Builds a House, Luella Connelly
				Night in the Barn, Faye Gibbons
				The Amazing Bone, William Steig
				The Gift, Marcia S. Freeman
				The Gingerbread Baby, Jan Brett
				The Great Kapok Tree: A Tale of the Amazon Rain Forest, Lynne Cherry

L	CR	BR	P	TRADE BOOK MODELS (cont.)
				The Hat, Jan Brett
				The Little Engine That Could, Watty Piper
				The Remarkable Farkle McBride, John Lithgow
				The Snowy Day, Ezra Jack Keats (Caldecott Award)
				The Very Busy Spider, Eric Carle
				Verdi, Janell Cannon
				We're Going on a Bear Hunt, Michael Rosen
				Who Says a Dog Goes Bow-Wow?, Hank De Zutter
				Wiggle Waggle, Jonathan London

L	CR	BR	P	EDUCATIONAL BOOK MODELS
				At the Farm, David M. Schwartz (CTP, *Look Once, Look Again Science Series)*
				Crocodile Tea, Marcia Vaughan (Rigby), Big Book
				Feeling Things, Allan Fowler (Children's Press), Big Book
				One Stormy Night, Joy Cowley (The Wright Group), Big Book
				Sound, Melvin Berger (Newbridge, *Early Science*), Big Book
				Sounds of the Farm, Kari Jenson Gold (Newbridge, *Discovery Links)*
				_____
				_____
				_____
				_____
				_____

Specificity

Good readers make text-to-self connections. An important way by which authors help them do this is through a writing-craft technique called **specificity**. Specificity means writing *Kmart* instead of *store,* or *tulip* instead of *flower.* By using specificity, you make your readers smile as they say to themselves, *"Oh, that's just like me!" "I have been there [done that, know that] too."*

We opened our lunch boxes. Surprise! A Hershey bar for each of us. And chicken sandwiches. Good lunch!
(*The Train to Lulu's,* Elizabeth Fitzgerald Howard)

Note:

- Specificity sometimes requires using proper nouns in place of common nouns. Thus, it can help reinforce the rules of capitalization.

- Specificity is a good revision tool for young writers. Example: Revising *"We took a field trip to the museum"* to *"We took a field trip to the Cincinnati Museum of Natural History."* Or, *"We ate breakfast"* becomes, *"We had pancakes with syrup and berries on top for breakfast."*

L	CR	BR	P	TRADE BOOK MODELS
				Amos & Boris, William Steig
				Ant Cities, Arthur Dorros
				Baby Whales Drink Milk, Barbara Juster Esbensen
				Because of Winn-Dixie, Kate DiCamillo (Newbery Award) **(intermediate)**
				Bunny Bungalow, Cynthia Rylant
				Catch the Wind!: All About Kites, Gail Gibbons
				Catfish and Spaghetti, Marcia S. Freeman **(intermediate)**
				Chester's Way, Kevin Henkes
				Chrysanthemum, Kevin Henkes
				Flood, Mary Calhoun
				Going West, Jean Van Leeuwen
				Make Way for Ducklings, Robert McCloskey
				Moja Means One: Swahili Counting Book, Muriel Feelings (Caldecott Award)
				Mrs. Mack, Patricia Polacco
				My Great-Aunt Arizona, Gloria Houston
				Paddle-to-the-Sea, Holling Clancy Holling
				Stuart Little, E. B. White **(intermediate)**
				Tales of a Fourth Grade Nothing, Judy Blume **(intermediate)**
				The Armadillo from Amarillo, Lynne Cherry **(intermediate)**

L	CR	BR	P

TRADE BOOK MODELS (cont.)

The Cookie-Store Cat, Cynthia Rylant

The Little Engine That Could, Watty Piper

The Night Before Christmas, Clement Moore

A Picture Book of Lewis and Clark, David A. Adler

Pottery Place, Gail Gibbons

The Train to Lulu's, Elizabeth Fitzgerald Howard

Town Mouse, Country Mouse, Jan Brett

Train Song, Diana Siebert

Whales, Cynthia Rylant

What Happens to a Hamburger?, Paul Showers

When I Was Young in the Mountains, Cynthia Rylant

Who Eats What? Food Chains and Food Webs, Patricia Lauber

L	CR	BR	P

EDUCATIONAL BOOK MODELS

A Rain Forest Adventure, Christine and Anton Economos (Newbridge, *Discovery Links*)

Conquering Mount Everest, Jackie Glassman (Benchmark, *Navigators*)

Desert Racers, Tracy Nelson Maurer (Rourke)

How Do You Know It's Spring?, Allan Fowler (Children's Press), Big Book

How Do You Know It's Winter?, Allan Fowler (Children's Press), Big Book

It Could Still Be a Rock, Allan Fowler (Children's Press) Big Book

Limousines, Tracy Nelson Maurer (Rourke)

Mexico City is Muy Grande, Marlene Perez (The Wright Group, *TWIG Books*)

Oceans, Katy Pike and Maureen O'Keefe (Newbridge, *Go Facts*)

People and the Sea, Sharon Dalgleish and Garda Turner (Newbridge, *Go Facts*)

The American Flag, Lynda Sorensen (Rourke)

Where Is My Continent?, Robin Nelson (Lerner Publishing, *First Avenue Editions*)

L	CR	BR	P

EDUCATIONAL BOOK MODELS (cont.)

_____

_____

_____

_____

_____

Other General Writing-Craft Skills

Alliteration

Good writers construct text with an ear for the sound of our language. For example, they deliberately put words in close proximity to one another that have similar *starting*, *medial*, or *ending* sounds. That technique, encompassing all configurations of word placement, is called **euphony**.

When we specifically put words together, or in close proximity, that start with the same consonant or consonant blend or end with a similar sound, we are using **alliteration**. When we put like-sounding words at the end of succeeding sentences, we are creating **rhyme**.

*The **curious cat crept** across the room and leaped onto the windowsill.*
   (student writing)

*You can hear the sounds of woodpeckers hammering **for food from far** away.*
   Informational expository text (*Getting Dinner*, Jennifer Blizin Gillis)

*Penguins **slide** and **glide** across the ice flow.*
   Informational text (*Puffins Climb, Penguins Rhyme*, Bruce McMillan)

*When Ned said, "giraffe," you could see a **giraffe**,*
*And its neck was so long it made everyone **laugh**.*
   (*Incredible Ned*, Bill Maynard)

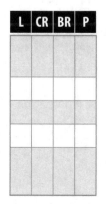

L	CR	BR	P

TRADE BOOK MODELS

A Pinky is a Baby Mouse: And Other Baby Animal Names, Pam Muñoz Ryan

Bees and Wasps, David Cutts

Big Al, Andrew Clements

Bunny Bungalow, Cynthia Rylant

Chicka Chicka Boom Boom, Bill Martin Jr. and John Archambault

L	CR	BR	P	TRADE BOOK MODELS (cont.)
				Commotion in the Ocean, Giles Andreae
				Crunch Munch, Jonathan London
				Goblins in Green, Nicholas Heller
				Happy Birthday, Moon, Frank Asch
				In November, Cynthia Rylant
				Incredible Ned, Bill Maynard
				Kate's Giants, Valiska Gregory
				Let's Go Home: The Wonderful Things About a House, Cynthia Rylant
				Night in the Barn, Faye Gibbons
				Off We Go!, Jane Yolen
				Puffins Climb, Penguins Rhyme, Bruce McMillan
				So You Want to Be President?, Judith St. George (Caldecott Award)
				The Cookie-Store Cat, Cynthia Rylant
				The Gift, Marcia S. Freeman
				The Hat, Jan Brett
				The Mitten, Jan Brett
				The Slippery Slope, Lemony Snicket (**intermediate**)
				The Ticky-Tacky Doll, Cynthia Rylant
				The Very Hungry Caterpillar, Eric Carle
				The Very Quiet Cricket, Eric Carle
				Time for Bed, Mem Fox
				Train Song, Diana Siebert
				Walter the Baker, Eric Carle
				What am I? Music!, Alain Crozon
				Where Once There Was a Wood, Denise Fleming
				Who am I?, Alain Crozon and Aurelie Lanchais

L	CR	BR	P	EDUCATIONAL BOOK MODELS
				At the Farm, David M. Schwartz (CTP, *Look Once, Look Again Science Series*)
				Desert Racers, Tracy Nelson Maurer (Rourke)

L	CR	BR	P

EDUCATIONAL BOOK MODELS (cont.)

Getting Dinner, Jennifer Blizin Gillis (Rourke, *Readers for Writers*)

Investigating Rocks, Natalie Lunis and Nancy White (Newbridge, *Early Science*), Big Book

Feeling Things, Allan Fowler (Children's Press), Big Book

Kakadu Jack, Brenda Parkes (Rigby), Big Book

Listen to This, Patty Whitehouse (Rourke, *Readers for Writers*)

Made of Metal, Patty Whitehouse (Rourke, *Readers for Writers*)

Mammal Moms, Marcia S. Freeman (Rourke, *Readers for Writers*)

Perfect Pretzels, Marcie Bovetz (The Wright Group, *TWIG Books*)

Slugs and Snails, Colin Walker (The Wright Group)

Sticky Stuff, Luana K. Mitten and Mary Wagner (Rourke, *Readers for Writers*)

The Seasons of the Year, Marcia S. Freeman (Rourke, *Readers for Writers*), Big Book

The Work Book, Marcia S. Freeman (Rourke, *Readers for Writers*), Big Book

Turtles Take Their Time, Allan Fowler (Children's Press), Big Book

Wetlands, Marcia S. Freeman (Newbridge, *Early Science*), Big Book

What Is Place Value?, J. E. Osborne (Newbridge, *Early Math*), Big Book

Yum! Yuck!, Michaela Morgan (Rigby), Big Book

Contrast

Writers use **contrast** for emphasis, to show an important relationship of one fact to another, or to just make their text more graceful and enjoyable. Young writers can practice using antonyms in a sentence to learn this writing-craft skill.

*How can one **little** dog give us such **big** problems?*
  (student writer)

In narrative, a short paragraph based on contrast may look like this student's:

*Whenever we went **up**, my face turned green. And whenever we went **down**, my face turned white.*
  (student writer)

In informational writing (See also **Expository, Informational Text Structure, Comparison** in **Chapter 3**), a paragraph with contrast text structure might look like this:

Living things reproduce. Plants make seeds or spores. Animals lay eggs or have live young.
  (*Is it Alive?*, Marcia S. Freeman)

See **Expository: Informational Text** in **Chapter 3** for information and a bibliography for models of comparison (this includes contrast) text structure.

L	CR	BR	P	TRADE BOOK MODELS
				Amos & Boris, William Steig
				Big Al, Andrew Clements
				Comet's Nine Lives, Jan Brett
				Fireflies in the Night, Judy Hawes
				I Love You the Purplest, Barbara Joosse
				Is There Life in Outer Space?, Franklyn M. Branley
				Johnny Appleseed, Steven Kellogg
				Land of the Dark, Land of the Light: The Arctic National Wildlife Refuge, Karen Pandell
				Little Cloud, Eric Carle
				Moja Means One: Swahili Counting Book, Muriel Feelings (Caldecott Award)
				My Mama Says There Aren't Any Zombies, Ghosts, Vampires, Creatures, Demons, Monsters, Fiends, Goblins, or Things, Judith Viorst

L	CR	BR	P

TRADE BOOK MODELS (cont.)

Pickles to Pittsburgh, Judi Barrett

So You Want to Be President?, Judith St. George (Caldecott Award)

Sun Up, Sun Down, Gail Gibbons

Super-Completely and Totally the Messiest, Judith Viorst

The Biggest, Best Snowman, Margery Cuyler

The Cloud Book, Tomie dePaola

The Gingerbread Baby, Jan Brett

The Library, Sarah Stewart

The Napping House Wakes Up, Audrey Wood

Tops & Bottoms, Janet Stevens (Caldecott Award)

When the Fly Flew In…, Lisa Westberg Peters

L	CR	BR	P

EDUCATIONAL BOOK MODELS

A Katydid's Life, Nic Bishop (The Wright Group, *TWIG Books*)

Air Around Us, Luana K. Mitten and Mary Wagner (Rourke, *Readers for Writers*)

Desert Racers, Tracy Nelson Maurer (Rourke)

Feeling Things, Allan Fowler (Children's Press), Big Book

Frogs and Toads and Tadpoles, Too!, Allan Fowler (Children's Press), Big Book

Getting Ready to Race, Susan Ring (Newbridge, *Discovery Links*)

It Could Still Be a Rock, Allan Fowler (Children's Press) Big Book

It's a Good Thing There Are Insects, Allan Fowler (Children's Press), Big Book

How Do You Know It's Winter?, Allan Fowler (Children's Press), Big Book

Life in the Sea, Melvin Berger (Newbridge, *Early Science*), Big Book

Made of Metal, Patty Whitehouse (Rourke, *Readers for Writers*)

L	CR	BR	P

EDUCATIONAL BOOK MODELS (cont.)

Polar Regions, Alison Ballance (Dominie Press)

Push and Pull, Marcia S. Freeman (Newbridge, *Early Science*), Big Book

Reptiles, Lynn Stone (Rourke, *Animals in Disguise*)

Short, Tall, Big or Small?, Kari Jenson Gold (Newbridge, *Early Math*)

So That's How the Moon Changes Shape!, Allan Fowler (Children's Press), Big Book

Spiders, Lisa Trumbauer (Newbridge, *Discovery Links*)

Sunflower, David M. Schwartz (CTP, *Life Cycles Science Series*)

The Seasons of the Year, Marcia S. Freeman (Rourke, *Readers for Writers*), Big Book

Turtles Take Their Time, Allan Fowler (Children's Press), Big Book

Wetlands, Marcia S. Freeman (Newbridge, *Early Science*), Big Book

What Plant is This?, Marcia S. Freeman (Rourke, *Readers for Writers*), Big Book

What's Alive?, Lisa Trumbauer (Newbridge, *Discovery Links*)

Woolly Sheep and Hungry Goats, Allan Fowler (Children's Press), Big Book

Yellow with Other Colors, Victoria Parker (Raintree, *Sprouts*)

_____

_____

_____

_____

_____

Embedded Definitions

Embedded definitions are a way by which writers of informational text save their readers from excessive trips to the glossary. (As evidenced by Lemony Snicket's work, the technique can be used in narrative as well). Content-area writers—science, math, history, geography, art, music, etc.—introduce their readers to many new words. They especially need to define some of these words *right in their* text so their readers can make some sense of what they are reading.

You can embed definitions in the text in a variety of ways:

- By defining something in **dictionary style**:
  Coil springs are long pieces of wire wound into a tube shape.
  (*Put It Together,* Patty Whitehouse)

- By saying what it is **made of**:
  A pattern is a design made up of parts that repeat again and again.
  (*Patterns in Nature,* Jennifer Blizin Gillis)

- By telling **what it does**:
  Meteorologists study the weather.
  (*Air Around Us,* Luana K. Mitten and Mary Wagner)

- By calling it **another more familiar name**, set off by commas, a dash, or the word *"or"*:
  *A gas, called carbon dioxide, comes in through the stomata, **or** tiny holes in the leaf.*
  (*Hurray for Plants,* Jennifer Blizin Gillis)

  Eagles use their claws, called talons, to grab their food.
  (*Getting Dinner,* Jennifer Blizin Gillis)

  The water flows in rivulets—small channels of moving water.
  (*Back to the Sea,* Patty Whitehouse)

L	CR	BR	P	**TRADE BOOK MODELS**
▓		▓		*An Octopus Is Amazing,* Patricia Lauber
				Animal Dads, Sneed B. Collard III
▓		▓		*Bees and Wasps,* David Cutts
				Catch the Wind!: All About Kites, Gail Gibbons
▓		▓		*Crow Boy,* Taro Yashima
				Dolphins, Tammy Everts and Bobbie Kalman
▓		▓		*Germs Make Me Sick!,* Melvin Berger
				King Bob's New Clothes, Dom DeLuise
▓		▓		*My Five Senses,* Aliki
				One Small Place by the Sea, Barbara Brenner
▓		▓		*Pottery Place,* Gail Gibbons
				Sharks, Seymour Simon
▓		▓		*The Armadillo from Amarillo,* Lynne Cherry **(intermediate)**
				The Honey Makers, Gail Gibbons

TRADE BOOK MODELS (cont.)

L	CR	BR	P	
				The Reptile Room, Lemony Snicket (**intermediate**)
				The Slippery Slope, Lemony Snicket (**intermediate**)
				The Underwater Alphabet Book, Jerry Pallotta
				Weather, Robyn Supraner
				What Happened to the Dinosaurs?, Franklyn M. Branley
				What Happens to a Hamburger?, Paul Showers

EDUCATIONAL BOOK MODELS

L	CR	BR	P	
				A Katydid's Life, Nic Bishop (The Wright Group, *Twig Books*)
				Amazing Crickets, Daniel Jacobs (Newbridge, *Discovery Links*)
				Amazing Rain Forest, Ted O'Hare (Rourke, *Rain Forests Today*)
				As Big As a Whale, Melvin Berger (Newbridge, *Ranger Rick*), Big Book
				Bean, David M. Schwartz (CTP, *Life Cycles Science Series*)
				Boas, Ted O'Hare (Rourke, *Amazing Snakes Discovery Library*)
				Dirt, Luana K. Mitten and Mary Wagner (Rourke, *Readers for Writers*)
				Everything Under the Sun, Marcia S. Freeman (Rourke, *Readers for Writers*), Big Book
				Frogs and Toads and Tadpoles, Too!, Allan Fowler (Children's Press), Big Book
				Fungi, Mary Kay Carson (Newbridge, *Ranger Rick*), Big Book
				Getting Dinner, Jennifer Blizin Gillis (Rourke, *Readers for Writers*)
				In the Garden, David M. Schwartz (CTP, *Look Once, Look Again Science Series*)
				It Could Still Be a Fish, Allan Fowler (Children's Press), Big Book
				It Could Still Be a Rock, Allan Fowler (Children's Press), Big Book

L	CR	BR	P

EDUCATIONAL BOOK MODELS (cont.)

It's a Good Thing There Are Insects, Allan Fowler (Children's Press), Big Book

Let's Look at Rocks, Luana K. Mitten and Mary Wagner (Rourke, *Readers for Writers*)

Perfect Pretzels, Marcie Bovetz (The Wright Group, *TWIG Books*)

Polar Regions, Alison Ballance (Dominie Press)

Rocks and Soil, Natalie Lunis (Newbridge, *Early Science*), Big Book

Sea Anemones, Lynn M. Stone (Rourke, *Science Under the Sea*)

Smart, Clean Pigs, Allan Fowler (Children's Press), Big Book

So That's How the Moon Changes Shape!, Allan Fowler (Children's Press), Big Book

Solid, Liquid or Gas?, Fay Robinson (The Wright Group, *TWIG Books*)

The Work Book, Marcia S. Freeman (Rourke, *Readers for Writers*), Big Book

Turtles Take Their Time, Allan Fowler (Children's Press), Big Book

Wetlands, Marcia S. Freeman (Newbridge, *Early Science*), Big Book

Woolly Sheep and Hungry Goats, Allan Fowler (Children's Press), Big Book

Young Geographers, Marcia S. Freeman (Rand McNally, *People, Spaces, and Places*), Big Book

_____

_____

_____

_____

_____

Clues for Readers to Make Inferences

Good readers think, and good writers stimulate them to do it. They do this by not telling their readers everything. Instead, they leave **clues** so the readers have to figure out some things for themselves.

That dog chases everyone. And be careful because he bites if you run. He bit my brother when he took off after delivering the newspaper.

The reader makes the inference: *"That is one mean dog."*

This writing technique enriches the text and engages the reader. Think how boring the above text would have been if the writer had just written, *"That dog is mean."* For more on this, refer to the **Don't Hit Your Reader Over the Head** lesson in my CraftPlus writing program and staff development resource, or my books, *Building a Writing Community* and *Teaching the Youngest Writers.*

> **Text-less books** and **riddle books** are also good models for teaching readers how to use clues to make inferences. In text-less books, the illustration provides the clues. Making inferences from pictures is a precursor skill to making inferences from text.

L	CR	BR	P	Trade Book Models
				Around the Pond: Who's Been Here?, Lindsay Barrett George
				Happy Birthday, Moon, Frank Asch
				Ida Early Comes Over the Mountain, Robert Burch **(intermediate)**
				Is Your Mama a Llama?, Deborah Guarino
				On Monday When It Rained, Cherryl Kachenmeister
				Miss Nelson is Back, Harry Allard and James Marshall
				Mrs. Mack, Patricia Polacco
				Night in the Barn, Faye Gibbons
				Scatterbrain Sam, Ellen Jackson
				The Gardener, Sarah Stewart
				The Gift, Marcia S. Freeman
				The Other Side, Jacqueline Woodson
				The Snowman, Raymond Briggs **(text-less)**
				Tuesday, David Wiesner **(text-less)**
				Two Bad Ants, Chris Van Allsburg
				Wanted...Mud Blossom, Betsy Byars
				When I Was Young in the Mountains, Cynthia Rylant
				When the Elephant Walks, Keiko Kasza
				Where Once There Was a Wood, Denise Fleming

L	CR	BR	P	EDUCATIONAL BOOK MODELS
				Among the Flowers, David M. Schwartz (CTP, *Look Once, Look Again Science Series*)
				Animal Homes, Susan Hartley and Shane Armstrong (Scholastic, *Reading Discovery*)
				At the Farm, David M. Schwartz (CTP, *Look Once, Look Again Science Series*)
				At Work, Margaret Mooney (Newbridge, *Discovery Links*)
				Dear Grandma, Avelyn Davidson (Shortland Publications, *Storyteller*)
				Giants, Wendy Blaxland (Scholastic, *Reading Discovery*)
				Graph It!, Jennifer Osborne (Newbridge, *Early Math*), Big Book
				In the Garden, David M. Schwartz (CTP, *Look Once, Look Again Science Series*)
				Is It Time?, Jane Campbell (Scholastic, *Reading Discovery*)
				Kakadu Jack, Brenda Parkes (Rigby), Big Book
				One Frog, One Fly, Wendy Blaxland (Scholastic, *Reading Discovery*)
				Solid Shapes, Kari Jenson Gold (Newbridge, *Early Math*), Big Book
				Wheels, Brian and Jillian Cutting (The Wright Group, *Sunshine Books*)
				Yum! Yuck!, Michaela Morgan (Rigby), Big Book
				_____
				_____
				_____
				_____
				_____

Riddle Books

Riddles are made up of clues. A reader infers the answer to the riddle by using those clues. Riddle books, therefore, make good models for teaching the craft skill of providing clues for inference.

Riddle clues are often descriptive: "*What has eight legs and weaves?*"

Use my sticks to beat, beat, beat. To my rhythm you'll march right down the street. What am I?
    (*What am I? Music!*, Alain Crozon)

L	CR	BR	P	TRADE BOOK MODELS
				Kindle Me a Riddle: A Pioneer Story, Roberta Karim
				Scatterbrain Sam, Ellen Jackson
				The Amazing I Spy ABC, Ken Laidlaw
				What am I? Music!, Alain Crozon
				Who am I?, Alain Crozon and Aurelie Lanchais

L	CR	BR	P	EDUCATIONAL BOOK MODELS
				What Hatches?, Don L. Curry (Capstone, *Yellow Umbrella Books)*
				Up Close, Brenda Parkes (Newbridge, *Discovery Links)*
				_____
				_____
				_____
				_____
				_____

Repetition

Writers of all genres use **repetition** both for emphasis and for the sound effect. They repeat words, phrases, or sentences.

So they drank up <u>all their pop</u> and ate up <u>all their crackers</u> and traveled up <u>all those miles</u> until finally they pulled into our yard.
    (*The Relatives Came*, Cynthia Rylant)

L	CR	BR	P	TRADE BOOK MODELS
				Africa Dream, Eloise Greenfield
				Bees and Wasps, David Cutts
				Brown Bear, Brown Bear, What Do You See?, Bill Martin Jr., and Eric Carle
				Chicken Sunday, Patricia Polacco
				Clifford and the Halloween Parade, Norman Bridwell
				Dinosaurs, Dinosaurs, Byron Barton

L	CR	BR	P

TRADE BOOK MODELS (cont.)

Does a Kangaroo Have a Mother, Too?, Eric Carle

Going West, Jean Van Leeuwen

Harriet, You'll Drive Me Wild!, Mem Fox

Hey! Get Off Our Train, John Burningham

Hush, Mingfong Ho

I Need a Lunch Box, Jeannette Caines and Pat Cummings

Is Your Mama a Llama?, Deborah Guarino

Just Because I Am a Child, Lauren Murphy Payne

Kate's Giants, Valiska Gregory

King Bob's New Clothes, Dom DeLuise

Land of the Dark, Land of the Light: The Arctic National Wildlife Refuge, Karen Pandell

Mike Mulligan and His Steam Shovel, Virginia Lee Burton

Mrs. Katz and Tush, Patricia Polacco

My Beautiful Child, Lisa Desimini and Matt Mahurin

My Five Senses, Aliki

My Great-Aunt Arizona, Gloria Houston

My Mama Says There Aren't Any Zombies, Ghosts, Vampires, Creatures, Demons, Monsters, Fiends, Goblins, or Things, Judith Viorst

Off We Go!, Jane Yolen

One Hundred Hungry Ants, Elinor J. Pinczes

Polar Bear, Polar Bear, What Do You Hear?, Bill Martin Jr.

"Slowly, Slowly, Slowly," Said the Sloth, Eric Carle

Stone Soup, Ann McGovern

Super-Completely and Totally the Messiest, Judith Viorst

Thanksgiving is…, Louise Borden

The Armadillo from Amarillo, Lynne Cherry **(intermediate)**

The Carrot Seed, Ruth Krauss

The Christmas Crocodile, Bonny Becker

The Gift, Marcia S. Freeman

The Gingerbread Baby, Jan Brett

L	CR	BR	P

TRADE BOOK MODELS (cont.)

The Gingerbread Man, Retold by Jim Aylesworth

The Giving Tree, Shel Silverstein

The Library, Sarah Stewart

The Little Engine That Could, Watty Piper

The Mitten, Jan Brett

The Napping House Wakes Up, Audrey Wood

The Relatives Came, Cynthia Rylant

The Reptile Room, Lemony Snicket (**intermediate**)

The Treasure, Uri Shulevitz

The Very Busy Spider, Eric Carle

The Witch Who Was Afraid of Witches, Alice Low

Time for Bed, Mem Fox

Tops & Bottoms, Janet Stevens (Caldecott Award)

Waiting For Sunday, Carol Blackburn

What Happens to a Hamburger?, Paul Showers

What Was I Scared Of?, Dr. Seuss

When I Was Little: A Four-Year-Old's Memoir of Her Youth, Jamie Lee Curtis

Where Once There Was a Wood, Denise Fleming

Why Mosquitoes Buzz in People's Ears, Verna Aardema (Caldecott Award)

L	CR	BR	P

EDUCATIONAL BOOK MODELS

Amazing Crickets, Daniel Jacobs (Newbridge, *Discovery Links)*

Amazing Rain Forest, Ted O'Hare (Rourke, *Rain Forests Today)*

Animals in Hiding, Melvin Berger (Newbridge, *Early Science*), Big Book

Clay Hernandez: A Mexican American, Diane Hoyt-Goldsmith (Newbridge)

Crocodile Tea, Marcia Vaughan (Rigby), Big Book

In the Garden, David M. Schwartz (CTP, *Look Once, Look Again Science Series*)

L	CR	BR	P

EDUCATIONAL BOOK MODELS (cont.)

Perfect Pretzels, Marcie Bovetz (The Wright Group, *TWIG Books*)

Solid, Liquid or Gas?, Fay Robinson (The Wright Group, *TWIG Books*)

Where Is My Continent?, Robin Nelson (Lerner Publishing, *First Avenue Editions*)

Yellow with Other Colors, Victoria Parker (Raintree, *Sprouts*)

Yum! Yuck!, Michaela Morgan (Rigby), Big Book

_____

_____

_____

_____

> Note: In your own writing, you may want to try using repetition as a transitional device to connect two successive sentences or paragraphs to each other. Start a second sentence or paragraph with the same word, phrase, or sentence that ended the preceding sentence or paragraph. Please note that this is an advanced literary technique for fluent writers, called anadiplosis. I mention it just for your information, for you to add to *your own* writing-craft expertise.
>
> *Lunch over, the two fifth graders huddled in the cafeteria. Paula looked over at Amelia and pronounced,*
> *"I hope I never see **that self-centered twit Jessica again.**"*
>
> ***The self-centered twit** sauntered out of the cafeteria. She stopped outside Mrs. Hull's classroom to glance at her reflection in the glass-fronted display case. Satisfied, she entered the room.*

Beginnings

You need to engage your readers whether you are writing fiction or non-fiction. You have to hook them early on. The first one or two sentences you write must attract their attention, be easy to read, and reveal the topic. To accomplish this, writers create **hooks** (also called leads or first lines), selecting one appropriate to the topic or the story from a large variety of techniques.

For instance, if your topic has noise associated with it, you may find onomatopoeia a useful hook. If your readers are going to learn by reading the text, you may want to start with a question that reflects what they will learn. If place is important to what you are describing, setting may be the appropriate hook. Fiction first lines or hooks are almost always tied closely to the main elements of character, setting, theme, or plot. Note also that some of these hook techniques may be combined.

You and your students can use the examples provided here to help you find other instances of the same techniques in your own readings. You should then add these books to the class or personal reference lists. The list of hook-techniques given here is by no means exhaustive, but it contains most of the common techniques professional writers use.

I recommend that you do not give your students the whole list in printed form, or even display it in your room in poster form. If you do, you will find that it is too long and that your students will not use it. Instead, provide them with a starter list of just a few techniques. Then have them add to it other hooks that they find in their independent reading.

There is no rule that dictates which of these techniques a writer should use in a given piece. The hook the writer chooses depends on his topic or his story and the technique he feels is the most effective.

1. Question

In a **question** hook, an author talks directly to her readers, asking a question designed to tweak their interest in the subject.

L	CR	BR	P	TRADE BOOK MODELS
				Do You Want To Be My Friend?, Eric Carle
				Is Your Mama a Llama?, Deborah Guarino
				Mojave, Diane Siebert
				Shoes from Grandpa, Mem Fox
				The Seashore Book, Charlotte Zolotow
				Weather, Robyn Supraner
				Where Are You Going? To See My Friend!, Eric Carle and Kazuo Iwamura

L	CR	BR	P	EDUCATIONAL BOOK MODELS
				A Bird's-Eye View, Marcia S. Freeman (Rand McNally, *People, Spaces, and Places*), Big Book

L	CR	BR	P

EDUCATIONAL BOOK MODELS (cont.)

Animals and Their Babies, Melvin Berger (Newbridge, *Early Science*), Big Book

At the Farm, David M. Schwartz (CTP, *Look Once, Look Again Science Series)*

At the Pond, Marcia S. Freeman (Rourke, *Readers for Writers*)

A World of Change, Natalie Lunis and Nancy White (Newbridge, *Early Science*), Big Book

Flavors From Plants, Jennifer Blizin Gillis (Rourke, *Readers* for Writers)

It's Best to Leave a Snake Alone, Allan Fowler (Children's Press), Big Book

Leaping Frogs, Melvin Berger (Newbridge, *Early Science*), Big Book

Limousines, Tracy Nelson Maurer (Rourke)

Made of Metal, Patty Whitehouse (Rourke, *Readers* for Writers)

Sorting It All Out, Luana K. Mitten and Mary Wagner (Rourke, *Readers for Writers*)

Summer, Katy Pike (Newbridge, *Go Facts*)

The World of Ants, Melvin Berger (Newbridge, *Early Science*), Big Book

Tundra, Lynn M. Stone (Rourke, *Biomes of North America*)

Turtles Take Their Time, Allan Fowler (Children's Press), Big Book

What Plant is This?, Marcia S. Freeman (Rourke, *Readers for Writers*), Big Book

2. Exclamation

Writers use **exclamations** to show that something exciting is happening, or that a particular fact is exciting to know. The writer hopes that the reader will get excited, too, and want to read on.

L	CR	BR	P

TRADE BOOK MODELS

My Hands, Aliki

Postcards From Pluto: A Tour of the Solar System, Loreen Leedy

Recycle!: A Handbook for Kids, Gail Gibbons

The Underwater Alphabet Book, Jerry Pallotta

L	CR	BR	P

EDUCATIONAL BOOK MODELS

Air Around Us, Luana K. Mitten and Mary Wagner (Rourke, *Readers for Writers*)

At Play in the Community, Judy Nayer (Newbridge, *Early Social Studies*), Big Book

Growing a Kitchen Garden, Natalie Lunis (Benchmark)

Frogs and Toads and Tadpoles, Too!, Allan Fowler (Children's Press), Big Book

Pasta, Please!, Melvin Berger (Newbridge, *Early Science*), Big Book

Sounds of the Farm, Kari Jenson Gold (Newbridge, *Discovery Links*)

Spinning a Web, Melvin Berger (Newbridge, *Early Science*), Big Book

Sunflower, David M. Schwartz (CTP, *Life Cycles Science Series*)

_____

_____

_____

_____

3. Startling fact

By using a **startling fact** to start a piece, the writer hopes to make the reader want to learn more about that fact. Of course, the writer must then provide the information that substantiates and explains the fact.

The blue whale is the biggest animal that ever lived. It is as long as three buses, as heavy as 25 elephants, and as tall as a two-story building.
  (*As Big As a Whale*, Melvin Berger)

L	CR	BR	P	TRADE BOOK MODELS
				A. Lincoln and Me, Louise Borden
				Chimps Don't Wear Glasses, Laura Joffe Numeroff
				Dogs Don't Wear Sneakers, Laura Joffe Numeroff
				Fossils Tell of Long Ago, Aliki
				Sharks, Seymour Simon
				Wackiest White House Pets, Kathryn Gibbs Davis
				What Do You Do When Something Wants to Eat You?, Steve Jenkins

L	CR	BR	P	EDUCATIONAL BOOK MODELS
				Amazing Rain Forest, Ted O'Hare (Rourke, *Rain Forests Today*)
				As Big As a Whale, Melvin Berger (Newbridge, *Ranger Rick*), Big Book
				Corals, Lynn M. Stone (Rourke, *Science Under the Sea*)
				Fungi, Mary Kay Carson (Newbridge, *Ranger Rick*), Big Book
				Getting Ready to Race, Susan Ring (Newbridge, *Discovery Links*)
				Insects, Katy Pike (Newbridge, *Go Facts*)
				Oceans, Katy Pike and Maureen O'Keefe (Newbridge, *Go Facts*)
				Pickles and Preserves, Judith Bauer Stamper (Newbridge, *Early Social Studies*), Big Book
				Rain Forest At Night, Ted O'Hare (Rourke, *Rain Forests Today*)
				Sea Anemones, Lynn M. Stone (Rourke, *Science Under the Sea*)
				Sponges, Lynn M. Stone (Rourke, *Science Under the Sea*)
				The Rockies, Mary Kay Carson (Newbridge, *Early Social Studies*), Big Book

L	CR	BR	P

EDUCATIONAL BOOK MODELS (cont.)

Solid, Liquid or Gas?, Fay Robinson (The Wright Group, *TWIG Books*)

_____

_____

_____

_____

_____

4. Statement of fact or opinion

Some authors jump right into their subject by making a **statement** or giving an **opinion** about it. No fancy leads for them! They are hoping that the cover of the book or its title has already hooked their readers. Once again, always remember that the writer is in charge.

The important thing about a spoon is that you eat with it.
  (*The Important Book*, Margaret Wise Brown)

L	CR	BR	P

TRADE BOOK MODELS

Apples, Gail Gibbons

Farming, Gail Gibbons

Fireflies in the Night, Judy Hawes

Mack Made Movies, Don Brown

Pigs, Gail Gibbons

Shoeless Joe and Black Betsy, Phil Bildner

Snakes Are Hunters, Patricia Lauber

So You Want to Be President?, Judith St. George (Caldecott Award)

The Important Book, Margaret Wise Brown

Whales, Gail Gibbons

L	CR	BR	P

EDUCATIONAL BOOK MODELS

All About Wood, Jennifer Prescott (Newbridge, *Early Social Studies*), Big Book

Boas, Ted O'Hare (Rourke, *Amazing Snakes Discovery Library*)

You Are a Scientist, Marcia S. Freeman (Rourke, *Readers for Writers*), Big Book

L	CR	BR	P	
				EDUCATIONAL BOOK MODELS (cont.)
				Building Things, Brian and Jillian Cutting (The Wright Group, *Sunshine Books)*
				Friction, Patty Whitehouse (Rourke, *Readers for Writers*)
				Making Mount Rushmore, Anastasia Suen (The Wright Group, *TWIG Books)*
				Mexico City is Muy Grande, Marlene Perez (The Wright Group, *TWIG Books)*
				Where Is My Continent?, Robin Nelson (Lerner Publishing, *First Avenue Editions)*
				_____
				_____
				_____
				_____
				_____

5. Setting (time or place)

Writers of story and expository alike sometimes use **setting** to start their pieces. They describe time or place in a creative way to tweak the reader's interest. Do the following tweak your interest?

An example from informational expository text:

Far beneath the ocean waves is an amazing world of odd creatures. Your parents didn't know a thing about it when they were your age. In fact, no one did!
    ("Weird World of the Deep," *Ranger Rick*, June 1998)

Two examples from fictional stories:

Maurice's room measured six long steps in one direction and five in the other.
    (*Maurice's Room*, Paula Fox)

On a small tropical island, the sun rose high above the steamy jungle.
    (*Verdi*, Janell Cannon)

L	CR	BR	P	
				TRADE BOOK MODELS
				Deserts, Gail Gibbons
				In November, Cynthia Rylant
				Kate's Giants, Valiska Gregory
				Manatee: On Location, Kathy Darling

L	CR	BR	P	TRADE BOOK MODELS (cont.)
				Maurice's Room, Paula Fox
				My Great-Aunt Arizona, Gloria Houston
				Owl Moon, Jane Yolen
				Polar Bears, Gail Gibbons
				Salt Hands, Jane Aragon
				The Biggest Bear, Lynd Ward
				The Crane's Gift, Steve and Megumi Biddle
				A Picture Book of Lewis and Clark, David A. Adler
				The Talking Eggs, Robert D. San Souci
				Verdi, Janell Cannon
				Whales, Cynthia Rylant
				Where Once There Was a Wood, Denise Fleming

L	CR	BR	P	EDUCATIONAL BOOK MODELS
				A Rain Forest Adventure, Christine and Anton Economos (Newbridge, *Discovery Links*)
				Backstage, Marcie Bovetz (The Wright Group, *TWIG BOOKS*)
				Conquering Mount Everest, Jackie Glassman (Benchmarks, *Navigators*) **(intermediate)**
				One Stormy Night, Joy Cowley (The Wright Group), Big Book
				_____
				_____
				_____
				_____
				_____

6. Definition

A **definition** may be just the thing to hook your reader. If, for example, the topic is revealed in the title, the author might need to let the reader know the definition of that topic.

If something is moved—lifted or lowered, pushed or pulled, blown or washed—work is being done. That is the scientific meaning of work.
  (*The Work Book*, Marcia S. Freeman)

L	CR	BR	P

TRADE BOOK MODELS

An Octopus Is Amazing, Patricia Lauber

Baby Whales Drink Milk, Barbara Juster Esbensen

Tunnels, Gail Gibbons

Who Eats What? Food Chains and Food Webs, Patricia Lauber

L	CR	BR	P

EDUCATIONAL BOOK MODELS

A Day, Robin Nelson (Lerner Publishing, *First Step)*

A Katydid's Life, Nic Bishop (The Wright Group, *TWIG Books)*

Birds, Paul McEvoy (Newbridge, *Go Facts*)

Fish, Katy Pike and Garda Turner (Newbridge, *Go Facts*)

Graph It!, Jennifer Osborne (Newbridge, *Early Math*) Big Book

Hurray for Plants, Jennifer Blizin Gillis (Rourke, *Readers for Writers*)

It's a Good Thing There Are Insects, Allan Fowler (Children's Press), Big Book

Inventions, Jennifer Osborne (Newbridge, *Early Science*), Big Book

Invertebrates, Lynn Stone (Rourke, *Animals in Disguise*)

Let's Do It Together, Denise M. Jordan (Heinemann, *Read and Learn)*

Life Cycle of a Monarch Butterfly, Jennifer Blizin Gillis (Rourke, *Readers for Writers*)

Map It!, Elspeth Leacock (Newbridge, *Early Social Studies*), Big Book

Patterns in Nature, Jennifer Blizin Gillis (Rourke, *Readers for Writers*)

Planes, Ian Rohr (Newbridge, *Go Facts*)

Reptiles, Lynn Stone (Rourke, *Animals in Disguise*)

The Web of Life, Melvin Berger (Newbridge, *Ranger Rick*), Big Book

The Work Book, Marcia S. Freeman (Rourke, *Readers for Writers*), Big Book

Trains, Ian Rohr (Newbridge, *Go Facts*)

L	CR	BR	P	EDUCATIONAL BOOK MODELS (cont.)
				_____
				_____
				_____
				_____
				_____

7. Onomatopoeia

If a writer uses **onomatopoeia** as a hook, naturally the sound has to be associated with the topic. If the writer starts with "BZZZZZZZZZZZZ," the reader expects to read about bees or humming birds, or something that buzzes.

"Arrah-arrah, arrah-arrah," noisy gannets call from the island cliffs. Some of them are telling the other birds, "This is my nest—stay away."
   ("Gawky, Squawky Gannets," *Ranger Rick*, February 1996)

L	CR	BR	P	TRADE BOOK MODELS
				Berlioz the Bear, Jan Brett
				Pancakes, Pancakes!, Eric Carle
				Peep!, Kevin Luthardt
				The Honey Makers, Gail Gibbons
				Seal Pup Grows Up: The Story of a Harbor Seal, Kathleen Weidner Zoehfeld
				The Little Engine That Could, Watty Piper

L	CR	BR	P	EDUCATIONAL BOOK MODELS
				Popcorn Science, Natalie Lunis and Nancy White (Newbridge, *Thinking Like a Scientist*), Big Book
				Signals for Safety, Nancy White (Newbridge, *Early Social Studies*), Big Book
				Sound, Melvin Berger (Newbridge, *Early Science*), Big Book
				_____
				_____
				_____
				_____

8. Alliteration

Alliteration and rhyme both produce pleasing sounds and are thus useful for getting a reader's attention. Some book titles take advantage of these literary devices: *Berlioz the Bear, Mack Made Movies, Make Mine Ice Cream,* and *Is Your Mama a Llama?*

Though we tell young writers not to write incomplete sentences, by fourth grade we can teach them that violating this prohibition can be an effective literary device, as long as it is done by design rather than by mistake. For example, stand-alone phrases, especially alliterative phrases, can produce effective and engaging hooks.

Sipping or slurping. Gripping or grabbing. Clawing or pawing. Animals get their food any way they can.

L	CR	BR	P	TRADE BOOK MODELS
				Bats, Gail Gibbons
				Leaf Jumpers, Carole Gerber
				The Moon Book, Gail Gibbons
				Planets, Gail Gibbons
				Stargazers, Gail Gibbons
				The Worrywarts, Pamela Duncan Edwards

L	CR	BR	P	EDUCATIONAL BOOK MODELS
				Exploring Everyday Wonders, Natatlie Lunis and Nancy White (Newbridge, *Thinking Like a Scientist*), Big Book
				People of the Rain Forest, Ted O'Hare (Rourke, *Rain Forests Today*)
				_____
				_____
				_____
				_____
				_____

9. Idioms

Idioms are figures of speech that act as language shortcuts. They are often metaphoric in nature. In the example below, author Pam Muñoz Ryan uses the idiomatic expression, "birds of a feather" to avoid a long explanation about the ways in which two of her characters are similar.

Amelia and Eleanor were birds of a feather.
   (*Amelia and Eleanor Go For a Ride*, Pam Muñoz Ryan)

Author Peggy Parish created her *Amelia Bedelia* books around the idea of idiom and Amelia's literal interpretation of words.

L	CR	BR	P

TRADE BOOK MODELS

Amelia and Eleanor Go For a Ride, Pam Muñoz Ryan

Clifford, We Love You, Norman Bridwell

Monkey Do!, Allan Ahlberg

_____

_____

_____

_____

10. Rhymes or Ditties

A **rhyme** or **ditty** an author uses may be one we all know, like the *"I scream, you scream. We all scream for ice cream"* that Melvin Berger used to begin *Make Mine Ice Cream.* But it may also be one that the author makes up.

L	CR	BR	P

TRADE BOOK MODELS

Duck, Duck, Goose!: (A Coyote's on the Loose!), Karen Beaumont

Shoes, Shoes, Shoes, Ann Morris

L	CR	BR	P

EDUCATIONAL BOOK MODELS

Make Mine Ice Cream, Melvin Berger (Newbridge, *Early Science*), Big Book

Solid Shapes, Kari Jenson Gold (Newbridge, *Early Math*), Big Book

The Money Book, Jennifer Osborne (Newbridge, *Early Math*), Big Book

What Is Place Value?, J. E. Osborne (Newbridge, *Early Math*), Big Book

Wheels, Brian and Jillian Cutting (The Wright Group, *Sunshine Books*)

EDUCATIONAL BOOK MODELS (cont.)

_____

_____

_____

_____

_____

11. Dialogue or a Quotation

To hook the reader, storywriters may start with a character speaking.

"C'mon, c'mon. Atta boy. Go on, take it!" Kerry leaned out over the bridge wall.
  (*Catfish and Spaghetti*, Marcia S. Freeman)

Expository writers may do so as well, perhaps by using a quotation from someone associated with the subject of the piece; for instance, *"Give me liberty or give me death"* to start a book about Patrick Henry. Or they may quote an expert in the subject of the piece, such as this start of an article about chemistry labs in schools: *"'Never use taste as a tool in the chemistry lab,' Dr. Graves advises his high school students."*

L	CR	BR	P	TRADE BOOK MODELS
				A Is For Abigail, Lynn Cheney
				Bigmama's, Donald Crews
				Billy's Picture, Margaret and HA Rey
				Catfish and Spaghetti, Marcia S. Freeman **(intermediate)**
				Daisy and the Egg, Jane Simmons
				Earrings!, Judith Viorst
				Flossie and the Fox, Pat McKissack
				Hey! Get Off Our Train, John Burningham
				Hurricane, David Wiesner
				Is Your Mama a Llama?, Deborah Guarino
				Mommy Go Away!, Lynne Jonell
				Sarah, Plain and Tall, Patricia MacLachlan
				Snowmen at Night, Caralyn Buehner
				Sunken Treasure, Gail Gibbons
				The Day Jimmy's Boa Ate the Wash, Trinka Hakes Nobel
				A Picture Book of Davy Crockett, David Adler

L	CR	BR	P	EDUCATIONAL BOOK MODELS
				Conquering Mount Everest, Jackie Glassman (Benchmark, *Navigators*)
				Crocodile Tea, Marcia Vaughan (Rigby), Big Book
				Perfect Pretzels, Marcie Bovetz (The Wright Group, *TWIG Books)*
				The American Flag, Lynda Sorensen (Rourke)
				So That's How the Moon Changes Shape!, Allan Fowler (Children's Press), Big Book
				Yum! Yuck!, Michaela Morgan (Rigby), Big Book

12. The name of a story character or a person associated with the topic

People like to read about people. Authors take advantage of that by naming a character central to a story or informational piece as a hook technique.

In a story:

My great-aunt Arizona was born in a log cabin her papa built in the meadow on Henson Creek in the Blue Ridge Mountains.
   (*My Great-Aunt Arizona,* Gloria Houston)

In an informational piece:

Meet Ranger Rick–Ranger Rick Hutchinson, that is! Rick loves his job at Yellowstone National Park. He started out as a ranger and now he's a scientist.
   ("Geyser Watcher," *Ranger Rick,* February 1996)

L	CR	BR	P	TRADE BOOK MODELS
				Because of Winn-Dixie, Kate DiCamillo (Newbery Award) **(intermediate)**
				Big Anthony and the Magic Ring, Tomie dePaola
				Big Panda, Little Panda, Joan Stimson
				Can't You Sleep, Little Bear?, Martin Waddell

L	CR	BR	P

TRADE BOOK MODELS (cont.)

Gert & Frieda, Anita Riggio

Henry and Beezus, Beverly Cleary

Mrs. Katz and Tush, Patricia Polacco

My Great-Aunt Arizona, Gloria Houston

Now One Foot, Now The Other, Tomie dePaola

Owl Babies, Martin Waddell

Phoebe's Revolt, Natalie Babbett

Sylvester and the Magic Pebble, William Steig

The Empty Pot, Demi

The Library, Sarah Stewart

The Treasure, Uri Shulevitz

Tico and the Golden Wings, Leo Lionni

Umbrella, Taro Yashima

Walter the Baker, Eric Carle

Wilfrid Gordon McDonald Partridge, Mem Fox

L	CR	BR	P

EDUCATIONAL BOOK MODELS

Why People Move, Margaret McNamara (Rand McNally, *People, Spaces, and Places*), Big Book

Where Do You Live?, Marcia S. Freeman (Rand McNally, *People, Spaces, and Places*), Big Book

_____

_____

_____

_____

_____

13. Description of a person: story character or a person in the article

A story or expository article can start with a **description** of the essential or predominant traits of the most important character or person in the piece. The description need only be as long as it takes to engage (hook) the reader. Here's one from a fictional story:

Dominic was a lively one, always up to something.
  (*Dominic*, William Steig)

L	CR	BR	P

TRADE BOOK MODELS

Badger's Parting Gifts, Susan Varley

Dominic, William Steig

Harriet, You'll Drive Me Wild!, Mem Fox

Harry the Dirty Dog, Gene Zion

Incredible Ned, Bill Maynard

Little Polar Bear and the Husky Pup, Hans de Beer

Piggie Pie!, Margie Palatini

Stuart Little, E. B. White (**intermediate**)

The Day Jake Vacuumed, Simon James

Tops & Bottoms, Janet Stevens (Caldecott Award)

Trashy Town, Andrea Zimmerman and David Clemesha

_____

_____

_____

_____

14. An event in progress

Describing an action can pique a reader's interest. The description need not be long. Indeed, all hooks are usually short. Its job is simply to get the reader's attention and reveal the topic.

An example from fiction (which uses specificity, by the way):

I won Dribble at Jimmy Fargo's birthday party.
  (*Tales of a Fourth Grade Nothing*, Judy Blume)

An example from informational text:

The plane bumps along the runway and rolls to a stop. My son, Anton, and I look out the plane window.
  (*The Rain Forest Adventure*, Christine and Anton Economos)

L	CR	BR	P

TRADE BOOK MODELS

Crow Boy, Taro Yashima

Encounter, Jane Yolen

Kindle Me a Riddle: A Pioneer Story, Roberta Karim

Little House on the Prairie, Laura Ingalls Wilder

Louie, Ezra Jack Keats

L	CR	BR	P	
				TRADE BOOK MODELS (cont.)
				Miss Nelson is Missing!, Harry Allard and James Marshall
				Oonawassee Summer, Melissa Forney (**intermediate**)
				Shiloh, Phyllis Reynolds Naylor (**intermediate**)
				Smoky Night, Eve Bunting
				Two Bad Ants, Chris Van Allsburg
				When the Fly Flew In…, Lisa Westberg Peters

L	CR	BR	P	
				EDUCATIONAL BOOK MODELS
				The Rain Forest Adventure, Christine and Anton Economos (Newbridge, *Discovery Links*)
				_____
				_____
				_____
				_____
				_____

15. Thoughts or action of a story character

Peter stretched as high as he could. There! His tall building was finished. CRASH!! Down it came.
    (*Peter's Chair*, Ezra Jack Keats)

L	CR	BR	P	
				TRADE BOOK MODELS
				Alexander, Who's Not (Do you hear me? I mean it!) Going to Move, Judith Viorst
				Froggy Goes to the Doctor, Jonathan London
				Froggy's Baby Sister, Jonathan London
				Moonbear's Pet, Frank Asch
				Peter's Chair, Ezra Jack Keats
				The Armadillo from Amarillo, Lynne Cherry (intermediate)
				The Raft, Jim LaMarche

L	CR	BR	P	
				EDUCATIONAL BOOK MODELS
				The Three Little Pigs, Brenda Parkes (Rigby), Big Book

L	CR	BR	P

EDUCATIONAL BOOK MODELS (cont.)

_____
_____
_____
_____
_____

16. Conflict

Authors sometimes hook their readers by setting up a **conflict** between characters or between characters and nature. This device is most often used in fiction, which is characterized and driven by plot. It might, however, also be used by a non-fiction writer who is reporting on or explaining a situation where there is an actual conflict: say, between two theories, two opposing opinions, or two suggested solutions to a problem.

In a story:

One Friday Miss Nelson told her class that she was going to have her tonsils out. "I'll be away next week," she said. "And I expect you to behave."
    (*Miss Nelson is Back*, Harry Allard and James Marshall)

L	CR	BR	P

TRADE BOOK MODELS

Henny Penny, Paul Galdone

Miss Nelson is Missing!, Harry Allard and James Marshall

Pigsty, Mark Teague

The Mitten, Jan Brett

The Missing Mitten Mystery, Steven Kellogg

Trouble with Trolls, Jan Brett

William's Doll, Charlotte Zolotow

_____
_____
_____
_____
_____

17. A letter or a note

A **letter** or a **note** may be used as a prologue to give the reader background information or to establish the plot. (See also **Chapter 3, Friendly Letters**).

L	CR	BR	P

TRADE BOOK MODELS

Pickles to Pittsburgh, Judi Barrett

Santa Domingo, Marguerite Henry (**intermediate**)

The Gardener, Sarah Stewart (Caldecott Award)

_____

_____

_____

_____

_____

Endings

You have probably seen some of your students just write *"The End"* when they thought they were finished with a piece. Unfortunately, doing that does not wrap things up for a reader. A reader needs a sense of closure, a feeling that the writer's thoughts or facts are completed. The writing-craft principle is: Don't leave your reader dangling.

Fiction writers end their stories by resolving the plot. Writers of personal narratives, which are plot-less, but not pointless, usually end their stories by summarizing their feelings, or noting a goal they reached or something they learned from the episode they have related. (See also **Chapter 3, Personal Narrative** and **Informational Narrative**).

Writers of expository text use a variety of ending techniques that summarize, remind, reiterate, question, or invite. Some of these endings hark back to, or echo, the hook. All provide closure for the reader.

And, as with beginning techniques, these ending techniques may be combined!

1. Question

Question endings act as an open invitation to the readers to learn more or to apply what they have learned in the book to new or future experiences. The question might also serve as a very short summary of the main idea.

Here's the final line in a book about what geographers (and young geographers studying geography) do:

We are young geographers. Are you?
   (*Young Geographers*, Marcia S. Freeman)

L	CR	BR	P

TRADE BOOK MODELS

Chimps Don't Wear Glasses, Laura Joffe Numeroff

Clifford, We Love You, Norman Bridwell

Crunch Munch, Jonathan London

Dogs Don't Wear Sneakers, Laura Joffe Numeroff

Is There Life in Outer Space?, Franklyn M. Branley

My Hands, Aliki

What Do You Do When Something Wants to Eat You?, Steve Jenkins

L	CR	BR	P

EDUCATIONAL BOOK MODELS

Backyard Scientist, Natalie Lunis (Newbridge, *Thinking Like a Scientist*), Big Book

Blood, Fay Robinson (The Wright Group, *TWIG Books*)

Building Strong Bridges, Kana Riley (The Wright Group, *TWIG Books*)

Feeling Things, Allan Fowler (Children's Press), Big Book

Getting Dinner, Jennifer Blizin Gillis (Rourke, *Readers for Writers)*

Going to the City, Marcia S. Freeman (Rand McNally, *People, Spaces, and Places*), Big Book

How Do You Know It's Winter?, Allan Fowler (Children's Press), Big Book

Investigating Rocks, Natalie Lunis and Nancy White (Newbridge, *Thinking Like a Scientist*), Big Book

Life in a Tree, Melvin Berger (Newbridge, *Early Science*), Big Book

Needs, Brenda Parkes (Newbridge, *Discovery Links*)

Where Do You Live?, Marcia S. Freeman (Rand McNally, *People, Spaces, and Places*), Big Book

Why People Move, Margaret McNamara (Rand McNally, *People, Spaces, and Places*), Big book

Why Polar Bears Like Snow…And Flamingos Don't, Nancy White (Benchmark, *Navigators*)

Young Geographers, Marcia S. Freeman (Rand McNally, *People, Spaces, and Places*), Big Book

L	CR	BR	P	EDUCATIONAL BOOK MODELS (cont.)
				_____
				_____
				_____
				_____
				_____

2. Exclamation

Authors sometimes use **exclamations** to add emphasis to their final statement about the subject of their book or piece. This emphasis can help give the reader a feeling of closure. This technique can be overdone, and beginning with the intermediate grades, students should be advised to make sure the ending statement merits an exclamation mark. The exclamatory ending statement may mimic the book's exclamatory hook.

L	CR	BR	P	TRADE BOOK MODELS
				Around the Pond: Who's Been Here?, Lindsay Barrett George
				Baby Whales Drink Milk, Barbara Juster Esbensen
				Germs Make Me Sick!, Melvin Berger
				How Do Apples Grow?, Betsy Maestro
				Helga's Dowry: A Troll Love Story, Tomie dePaola
				How I Spent My Summer Vacation, Mark Teague
				I Need a Lunch Box, Jeannette Caines and Pat Cummings
				On the Day You Were Born, Debra Fraiser
				Outside and Inside Sharks, Sandra Markle
				Recycle!: A Handbook for Kids, Gail Gibbons
				Stargazers, Gail Gibbons
				The Hat, Jan Brett
				The Missing Mitten Mystery, Steven Kellogg
				The Pumpkin Book, Gail Gibbons
				The Underwater Alphabet Book, Jerry Pallotta
				Time for Bed, Mem Fox
				When I Was Little: A Four-Year-Old's Memoir of Her Youth, Jamie Lee Curtis

L	CR	BR	P

TRADE BOOK MODELS (cont.)

Who Hops?, Katie Davis

L	CR	BR	P

EDUCATIONAL BOOK MODELS

Animal Covers, Luana K. Mitten and Mary Wagner (Rourke, *Readers for Writers*)

Backstage, Marcie Bovetz (The Wright Group, *TWIG Books*)

Do You Know It's Spring?, Allan Fowler (Children's Press), Big Book

Frogs and Toads and Tadpoles, Too!, Allan Fowler (Children's Press), Big Book

How Do You Know It's Spring?, Allan Fowler (Children's Press), Big Book

Hurray for Plants, Jennifer Blizin Gillis (*Readers for Writers*)

It Could Still Be a Fish, Allan Fowler (Children's Press), Big Book

Perfect Pretzels, Marcie Bovetz (The Wright Group, *TWIG Books*)

Snap Likes Gingersnaps, Rachel Gosset (Scholastic, *Reading Discovery*)

Solid Shapes, Kari Jenson Gold (Newbridge, *Early Math*), Big Book

The Barbecue, Jillian Cutting (The Wight Group, *Sunshine Books*)

Turtles Take Their Time, Allan Fowler (Children's Press), Big Book

Yellow with Other Colors, Victoria Parker (Raintree, *Sprouts*)

Yum! Yuck!, Michaela Morgan (Rigby), Big Book

_____

_____

_____

_____

_____

3. Universal word

The **universal-word** ending technique uses a word in the last sentence or two such as, *every, everything, everyone, everywhere, all, always, we, us,* and *all the world.* These words create a generalizing statement that summarizes the author's feelings about the subject, or which states the overall thought the writer wants the reader to take away.

*I go fishing with my Dad. We usually fish in a brook near our house. We don't even care if we catch anything. I could go fishing **every day**.*

L	CR	BR	P	TRADE BOOK MODELS
				A. Lincoln and Me, Louise Borden
				Hershel and the Hanukkah Goblins, Eric Kimmel
				Land of the Dark, Land of the Light: The Arctic National Wildlife Refuge, Karen Pandell
				Manatee: On Location, Kathy Darling
				Off We Go!, Jane Yolen
				One Small Place by the Sea, Barbara Brenner
				Out of the Ocean, Debra Fraiser
				Shoes, Shoes, Shoes, Ann Morris
				So You Want to Be President?, Judith St. George (Caldecott Award)
				Sylvester and the Magic Pebble, William Steig
				The Biggest Bear, Lynd Ward
				The Wednesday Surprise, Eve Bunting
				Wackiest White House Pets, Kathryn Gibbs Davis
				Weather, Robyn Supraner
				What Daddies Do Best, Laura Joffe Numeroff
				What Mommies Do Best, Laura Joffe Numeroff

L	CR	BR	P	EDUCATIONAL BOOK MODELS
				Animal Lives, Marcia S. Freeman (Rourke, *Readers for Writers*), Big Book
				Design It! Build It!, Susan Ring (Newbridge, *Early Science*), Big Book
				Everything Under the Sun, Marcia S. Freeman (Rourke, *Readers for Writers*) Big Book

L	CR	BR	P	EDUCATIONAL BOOK MODELS (cont.)
				From the Factory, Nancy White (Newbridge, *Early Social Studies*), Big Book
				Getting Ready to Race, Susan Ring (Newbridge, *Discovery Links*)
				It's Best to Leave a Snake Alone, Allan Fowler (Children's Press), Big Book
				Light, Melvin Berger (Newbridge, *Early Science*), Big Book
				People Everywhere, Jeri Cipriano (Newbridge, *Discovery Links*)
				Polar Regions, Alison Ballance (Dominie Press)
				Spiders, Lisa Trumbauer (Newbridge, *Discovery Links*)
				The Rain Forest, Melvin Berger (Newbridge, Ranger Rick), Big Book
				The Work Book, Marcia S. Freeman (Rourke, *Readers for Writers*), Big Book
				Trains, Ian Rohr (Newbridge, *Go Facts*)
				Where Does All The Garbage Go?, Melvin Berger (Newbridge, *Early Science*), Big Book
				You Are a Scientist, Marcia S. Freeman (Rourke, *Readers for Writers*), Big Book

4. Advice to the reader

Writers of fiction and non-fiction often have a final word of **advice** for the reader. Fables end with *a moral of the story*, which is often advice. Informational text writers sometimes use this ending technique to summarize the information in their piece.

So, the next time you bird-watch in Central Park, check the website, www. nycbirdreport.com for the location of unusual sightings.

L	CR	BR	P	TRADE BOOK MODELS
				Ant Cities, Arthur Dorros

L	CR	BR	P

TRADE BOOK MODELS (cont.)

Check It Out!: The Book About Libraries, Gail Gibbons

Little Red Riding Hood: A Newfangled Prairie Tale, Lisa Campbell Ernst

Sharks, Seymour Simon

So You Want to Be President?, Judith St. George (Caldecott Award)

L	CR	BR	P

EDUCATIONAL BOOK MODELS

All About Wood, Jennifer Prescott (Newbridge, *Early Social Studies*), Big Book

Bicycles, Morgan Hughes (Rourke, *Wheels in Motion*)

Desert Racers, Tracy Nelson Maurer (Rourke)

It Could Still Be a Tree, Allan Fowler (Children's Press), Big Book

Limousines, Tracy Nelson Maurer (Rourke)

Popcorn Science, Natalie Lunis and Nancy White (Newbridge, *Thinking Like a Scientist*), Big Book

_____

_____

_____

_____

_____

5. Reminder

A **reminder** to the reader is another technique writers of informational text use to summarize their main ideas.

Remember that while the porcupine will not "throw" its quills at you, do not try to pick one up. The barbs of the quills make it very difficult to pull them out.

L	CR	BR	P

TRADE BOOK MODELS

My Visit to the Aquarium, Aliki

The Cloud Book, Tomie dePaola

Super-Completely and Totally the Messiest, Judith Viorst

L	CR	BR	P

EDUCATIONAL BOOK MODELS

Being a Scientist, Natalie Lunis and Nancy White (Newbridge, *Thinking Like a Scientist*), Big Book

It's a Good Thing There Are Insects, Allan Fowler (Children's Press), Big Book

Let's Experiment, Natalie Lunis and Nancy White (Newbridge, *Thinking Like a Scientist*), Big Book.

Smart, Clean Pigs, Allan Fowler (Children's Press), Big Book

So That's How the Moon Changes Shape!, Allan Fowler (Children's Press), Big Book

What Do We Pay For?, Marilyn J. Salomon (Newbridge, *Early Social Studies*), Big Book

_____

_____

_____

_____

_____

6. Adage or Homily

An **adage** or **homily** is a short and pithy saying, such as, "*A penny saved is a penny earned.*" Or, "*Better safe than sorry.*" You may sometimes find them at the end of essays, fables, and even informational articles.

"Now my wings are black," I thought, "and yet I am not like my friends. We are all different. Each for his own memories, and his own invisible golden dreams."
   (*Tico and the Golden Wings*, Leo Lionni)

L	CR	BR	P

TRADE BOOK MODELS

Tico and the Golden Wings, Leo Lionni

L	CR	BR	P

EDUCATIONAL BOOK MODELS

The Money Book, Jennifer Osborne (Newbridge, *Early Math*), Big Book

The Three Little Pigs, Brenda Parkes (Rigby), Big Book

_____

_____

L	CR	BR	P

EDUCATIONAL BOOK MODELS (cont.)

_____
_____
_____

7. Quotation

Just as writers use quotations as a hook technique to engage their readers, they also sometimes use quotations to end a piece. The quotation should in some way sum up the essence of the text. Usually the quote is by someone featured in the article or by some noted person or authority.

At the end of text about fire safety:

…A final reminder from Fire Chief Mike Daley, "Remember, do not try to put a fire out on your own. Call 911."

L	CR	BR	P

TRADE BOOK MODELS

America: A Patriotic Primer, Lynn Cheney

Apples to Oregon, Deborah Hopkinson and Nancy Carpenter

L	CR	BR	P

EDUCATIONAL BOOK MODELS

Conquering Mount Everest, Jackie Glassman (Benchmark, *Navigators*)

_____
_____
_____
_____

8. End of a process or cycle

Life cycles, directions, and process descriptions are all sequentially organized genres. They usually end with the last step in the sequence. They also may end by **circling back to the hook** (See Item **9.**, immediately following).

L	CR	BR	P

TRADE BOOK MODELS

Cactus Hotel, Brenda Z. Guiberson

L	CR	BR	P

TRADE BOOK MODELS (cont.)

Seal Pup Grows Up: The Story of a Harbor Seal, Kathleen Weidner Zoehfeld

Sun Up, Sun Down, Gail Gibbons

L	CR	BR	P

EDUCATIONAL BOOK MODELS

A Butterfly is Born, Melvin Berger (Newbridge, *Early Science*), Big Book

Building Roads, Judith Bauer Stamper (Newbridge, *Early Social Studies*), Big Book

Cooking and Change, Paul McEvoy (Newbridge, *Go Facts*)

From Farms to You, Paul McEvoy (Newbridge, *Go Facts*)

Make Mine Ice Cream, Melvin Berger (Newbridge, *Early Science*), Big Book

Pumpkin Time, Luana K. Mitten and Mary Wagner (Rourke, *Readers for Writers*)

Squirrels All Year Long, Melvin Berger (Newbridge, *Early Science*)

_____

_____

_____

_____

_____

9. Circle back to the hook

Circling back to the hook means using a technique at the end that is similar to the one used as a beginning. The writer may use a variation of the hook, allude to the beginning, answer the question asked, and so forth.

Cobwebs in your telescope? Could be—no matter how often you dust. [The first sentence.]

[Mid-section of the article, which is about the crosshairs in telescopes.]

Cobwebs in your next telescope? Not likely unless you left the lens cap off. [The last sentence.]

    ("Cobwebs to Crosshairs," Carol Ann Moorhead, reprinted in *Listen to This* by Marcia S. Freeman)

And:

What happened to the dinosaurs? [The first sentence.]

[Rest of the article.]

Why the dinosaurs disappeared is still a mystery. [The last sentence.]
  (*What Happened to the Dinosaurs?*, Franklyn M. Branley)

L	CR	BR	P	TRADE BOOK MODELS
				Animals and Their Colors, Stephanie Maze
				Bees and Wasps, David Cutts
				Comet's Nine Lives, Jan Brett
				Country Crossing, Jim Aylesworth
				Dinosaurs, Dinosaurs, Byron Barton
				Growing Frogs, Vivian French
				If You Give a Moose a Muffin, Laura Joffe Numeroff
				If You Give a Mouse a Cookie, Laura Joffe Numeroff
				If You Give a Pig a Pancake, Laura Joffe Numeroff
				I Loved You Before You Were Born, Anne Bowen
				I Wish I Were a Butterfly, James Howe
				Mack Made Movies, Don Brown
				Mapping Penny's World, Loreen Leedy
				Monarch Butterflies, Gail Gibbons
				Morning, Noon, and Night, Jean Craighead George
				Mr. Willowby's Christmas Tree, Robert Barry
				Ox-Cart Man, Donald Hall
				Paddle-to-the-Sea, Holling Clancy Holling
				Raccoons and Ripe Corn, Jim Arnosky
				Snakes Are Hunters, Patricia Lauber
				The Honey Makers, Gail Gibbons
				Waiting for Wings, Lois Ehlert
				What Charlie Heard, Mordicai Gerstein
				What Happened to the Dinosaurs?, Franklyn M. Branley

L	CR	BR	P	EDUCATIONAL BOOK MODELS
				A Katydid's Life, Nic Bishop (The Wright Group, *TWIG Books*)

L	CR	BR	P	
				EDUCATIONAL BOOK MODELS (cont.)
				Conquering Mount Everest, Jackie Glassman (Benchmark, *Navigators*)
				Is It Time?, Jane Campbell (Scholastic, *Reading Discovery*)
				Mexico City is Muy Grande, Marlene Perez (The Wright Group, *TWIG Books*)
				Sharing News, Cynthia Rothman (Newbridge, *Discovery Links*)
				Solid, Liquid or Gas?, Fay Robinson (The Wright Group, *TWIG Books*)
				What Hatches?, Don L. Curry (Capstone, *Yellow Umbrella Books*)

_____

_____

_____

_____

_____

Sentence Variation

Writers need to keep their readers engaged. A good way to achieve this is by varying sentence form and length. Gary Provost, in his classic non-fiction writing guide, *100 Ways to Improve Your Writing*, cleverly illustrates what happens when writers do not vary sentence length.

This sentence has five words. Here are five more. Five-word sentences are fine. But several together become monotonous. Listen to what is happening. The writing is getting boring. The sound of it drones. It's like a stuck record.

Young writers can vary the length of their sentences by adding phrases and clauses to extend a sentence (to provide more information or detail), by constructing compound sentences, or by beginning sentences with *"And," "But,"* or *"Or."* Teach them that such techniques will help them keep their readers awake.

L	CR	BR	P	
				TRADE BOOK MODELS
				An Octopus Is Amazing, Patricia Lauber
				Because of Winn-Dixie, Kate DiCamillo (Newbery Award)

L	CR	BR	P

TRADE BOOK MODELS (cont.)

Boo to a Goose, Mem Fox

Fireflies in the Night, Judy Hawes

Fossils Tell of Long Ago, Aliki

In November, Cynthia Rylant

Is There Life in Outer Space?, Franklyn M. Branley

My Great-Aunt Arizona, Gloria Houston

Stellaluna, Janell Cannon

Nasty, Stinky Sneakers, Eve Bunting

The Mitten, Jan Brett

L	CR	BR	P

EDUCATIONAL BOOK MODELS (cont.)

Among the Flowers, David M. Schwartz (CTP, *Look Once, Look Again Science Series*)

Animal Lives, Marcia S. Freeman (Rourke, *Readers for Writers*), Big Book

Graph It!, Jennifer Osborne (Newbridge, *Early Math*), Big Book

How Do You Know It's Spring?, Allan Fowler (Children's Press), Big Book

Roaring Rides, Tracy Nelson Maurer (Rourke Classroom Resources/Library Collection)

The American Flag, Lynda Sorensen (Rourke Classroom Resources/Library Collection)

What Is Place Value?, J. E. Osborne (Newbridge, Early Math), Big Book

You Are a Scientist, Marcia S. Freeman (Rourke, *Readers for Writers*), Big Book

_____

_____

_____

_____

Voice Techniques

Voice is difficult to define precisely. It is made up of many components that together account for the uniqueness of each writer's language, his written fingerprint, if you will. It manifests itself in the words the author chooses, the tone he takes, the way he talks to his reader, the details he presents as important, the imagery he creates, and the rhythm of his writing.

We can teach young writers several specific techniques that will help them develop their voices as they practice writing craft, read well-written text, and gain experience and vocabulary. Some of the voice techniques we can readily address in elementary school are:

1. Using personal pronouns

Talking directly to the reader with the use of the **pronouns** "you," "I," and "we," or asking the reader a question. This technique is another tool the writer uses to engage his reader.

Happily, whales still live in all the world's oceans. Some day you may take a whale watching boat on the Atlantic or Pacific coast. Look for the telltale spout of a whale. Then you can cry out, "Thar she blows!"
   (*As Big As a Whale*, Melvin Berger)

Do the veins in the leaf look like the lines in the palm of your hand or like a feather?
   (*What Plant Is This?*, Marcia S. Freeman)

L	CR	BR	P	TRADE BOOK MODELS
				A Pinky is a Baby Mouse: And Other Baby Animal Names, Pam Muñoz Ryan
				Animal Dads, Sneed B. Collard III
				Are You a Snail?, Judy Allen
				Bats!: Strange and Wonderful, Laurence Pringle
				Big Al, Andrew Clements
				Brave Irene, William Steig
				Bunny Bungalow, Cynthia Rylant
				Canoe Days, Gary Paulsen
				Germs Make Me Sick!, Melvin Berger
				How I Became a Pirate, Melinda Long
				Library Lil, Suzanne Williams
				My Mama Says There Aren't Any Zombies, Ghosts, Vampires, Creatures, Demons, Monsters, Fiends, Goblins, or Things, Judith Viorst

L	CR	BR	P

TRADE BOOK MODELS (cont.)

One Small Place by the Sea, Barbara Brenner

So You Want to Be President?, Judith St. George (Caldecott Award)

Tar Beach, Faith Ringgold

The Great Gracie Chase: Stop That Dog!, Cynthia Rylant

The Slippery Slope, Lemony Snicket **(intermediate)**

The Ticky-Tacky Doll, Cynthia Rylant

The True Story of the 3 Little Pigs, Jon Scieszka

Who Eats What? Food Chains and Food Webs, Patricia Lauber

L	CR	BR	P

EDUCATIONAL BOOK MODELS

Acids and Bases, Lisa Benjamin (Newbridge, *Ranger Rick*), Big Book

As Big As a Whale, Melvin Berger (Newbridge, *Ranger Rick*), Big Book

Animal Covers, Luana K. Mitten and Mary Wagner (Rourke, *Readers for Writers*)

Friction, Patty Whitehouse (Rourke, *Readers for Writers*)

From Farms to You, Paul McEvoy (Newbridge, *Go Facts*)

Fungi, Mary Kay Carson (Newbridge, *Ranger Rick*), Big Book

Getting Dinner, Jennifer Blizin Gillis (Rourke, *Readers for Writers*)

Growing a Kitchen Garden, Natalie Lunis (Benchmark, *Navigators*)

I Can Be an Author, Ray Broekel (Children's Press)

In the Garden, David M. Schwartz (CTP, *Look Once, Look Again Science Series*)

Let's Do It Together, Denise M. Jordan (Heinemann, *Read and Learn*)

Made of Metal, Patty Whitehouse (Rourke, *Readers for Writers*)

Perfect Pretzels, Marcie Bovetz (The Wright Group, *TWIG Books*)

President's Day, Mir Tamim Ansary (Heinemann Library)

L	CR	BR	P	

EDUCATIONAL BOOK MODELS (cont.)

People and the Sea, Sharon Dalgleish and Garda Turner (Newbridge, *Go Facts*)

Shorebirds, Melissa Stewart (Newbridge, *Ranger Rick*), Big Book

Should There Be Zoos?, Tony Stead with students (Mondo), Big Book

What Is Place Value?, J. E. Osborne (Newbridge, *Early Math*), Big Book

What Plant is This?, Marcia S. Freeman (Rourke, *Readers for Writers*), Big Book

Why Polar Bears Like Snow…And Flamingos Don't, Nancy White (Benchmark, *Navigators*)

You Are a Scientist, Marcia S. Freeman (Rourke, *Readers for Writers*), Big Book

2. Aside to the Reader

Speaking in an **aside to the reader** is a way to make an editorial comment about what you have written.

A raccoon is a good fisherman. His paws are as fast as lightning. **You have to be quick with your hands to catch a fish.** [the aside]
    (student writer)

L	CR	BR	P	

TRADE BOOK MODELS

Bunny Bungalow, Cynthia Rylant

Going West, Jean Van Leeuwen

James and the Giant Peach, Roald Dahl

The Great Gracie Chase: Stop That Dog!, Cynthia Rylant

The Cookie-Store Cat, Cynthia Rylant

The Grim Grotto, Lemony Snicket (**intermediate**)

The Reptile Room, Lemony Snicket (**intermediate**)

The Slippery Slope, Lemony Snicket (**intermediate**)

L	CR	BR	P

TRADE BOOK MODELS (cont.)

The Ticky-Tacky Doll, Cynthia Rylant

Walter the Baker, Eric Carle

L	CR	BR	P

EDUCATIONAL BOOK MODELS

You Are a Scientist, Marcia S. Freeman (Rourke, *Readers for Writers*), Big Book

_____

_____

_____

_____

Chapter Three

THE GENRES AND THEIR ASSOCIATED WRITING-CRAFT SKILLS

■ ■

This chapter lists models for the genres that most K-8 student writers are required to write. These genres include narrative (personal narrative, informational narrative, and fiction), expository (informational, including variations in its text structure; personal expository; and persuasion), and friendly letters (narrative and expository). In order to develop your students' ears for each of the genres, your read-aloud choices should include a balance of all of them.

Narrative

Narrative, informally referred to as **story**, is characterized by a chronological ordering of events in which people or animals interact in a setting. Time passes in a story. In **fiction**, the plot drives the story. In **personal and informational narrative,** the writer's point—*why I am telling you this story*—drives the story.

Writers usually use the past tense for narrative but may occasionally use the present tense. They indicate changes in time and place with cues such as, *In the afternoon*, or *Meanwhile, back at the ranch.* They also flag these changes, as well as changes of action or speaker, by indenting to form new paragraphs. Narrative writers use engaging beginning and ending techniques and great descriptive imagery to create interesting and entertaining stories.

Some narratives are mainly informational, with the information woven into a chronologically ordered story. Many of Joanna Cole's *Magic School Bus* books take this form. A book about a family's journey into the Grand Canyon might be crammed full of information about the geology of the canyon. But this informational content does not change the narrative structure of the text: *It is still a narrative because it is organized chronologically, with time passing as the text progresses.*

Narrative writers use both **genre-specific skills**, such as time cues or dialogue tags, and **general skills**, such as strong verbs or literary devices. In this section, the various narrative genres are described, followed by the writing-craft skills that are specific to each. Refer back to **Chapter 2** for literature models of the general skills

Personal Narrative

Personal narratives are not plot-driven as fiction and plays are. But personal narratives *are* stories and they do have a point or focus. That point or focus might be an emotion, an accomplishment, a lesson learned, or a reflection about oneself or one's life that derives from the event. Personal narratives are the stories we often cherish and save to tell our grandchildren.

Like all narratives, personal narratives are organized in chronological order. Many of them also illustrate the "snake-that-ate-the-rat" shape—that is, they have short beginnings and endings and an elaborated middle consisting of a rich description of the main event. Personal narratives are always written in the first person. To enrich their stories, authors often aggrandize them with events and conversations that did not necessarily happen exactly as they relate them. In this regard, William Zinsser titled his book about writing memoir, *Inventing the Truth*.

Children's picture books written in the first person make good models for personal-narrative writing at any grade level. These first-person narratives are not authored by children, but the authors have written them from the perspective of their childhoods.

In kindergarten and first-grade classes, you should read many personal narratives to your students and help them identify and articulate the ending that drives the story: most often, the author's feelings about the event, or what she accomplished or learned. *But do not ask these students to write their own personal narratives until they can sequence events in time order*—an ability that they usually develop in late first grade and master in second grade.

To read about personal and informational expository genres and see how these genres are related to primary students' first writings, please refer to **II. Expository** in this chapter.

In Grades two–eight, continue to read personal narratives to your students to reiterate the chronological organization and to show them the elaboration techniques that writers use. Help them identify the ending that drives the story: the author's feelings or something the author achieved or learned, or a reflection about their own lives based on a text-to-self connection. I recommend that you select personal narrative as the first genre you teach students after starting the school year with instruction in descriptive writing.

L	CR	BR	P

TRADE BOOK MODELS

All Those Secrets of the World, Jane Yolen

Always My Dad, Sharon Dennis Wyeth

Best Friends, Steven Kellogg

L	CR	BR	P	TRADE BOOK MODELS (cont.)
				Galimoto, Karen Lynn Williams
				Grandfather's Journey, Allen Say (Caldecott Award)
				How I Spent My Summer Vacation, Mark Teague
				I Was Born About 10,000 Years Ago, Steven Kellogg
				Mrs. Mack, Patricia Polacco
				On Monday When It Rained, Cherryl Kachenmeister
				Our Teacher's Having a Baby, Eve Bunting
				Raising Yoder's Barn, Jane Yolen
				Roxaboxen, Alice McLerran
				Tell Me Again About the Night I Was Born, Jamie Lee Curtis
				The Carousel, Liz Rosenberg
				The Log of Christopher Columbus, Christopher Columbus (selections by Steve Lowe)
				The Other Side, Jacqueline Woodson
				The Relatives Came, Cynthia Rylant
				The Storm, Anne Rockwell
				The Train to Lulu's, Elizabeth Fitzgerald Howard
				Three Days on a River in a Red Canoe, Vera B. Williams

_____

_____

_____

_____

_____

Informational Narrative

Informational narratives are stories crammed full of information. Writers use this approach because they know we all love stories and it is therefore an entertaining and engaging way to present information. Student writers may want to try using this genre themselves as an alternative to a report.

All the general writing-craft skills covered in Chapter 2 apply to this genre. That is, the writer must provide imagery, engage the reader, provide for inference, and present the material in an organized fashion. But since the piece is a story, the writer must also use narrative-specific craft such as time, place, action, and speaker transitions if he uses dialogue.

The plane bumps along the runway and rolls to a stop. My son, Anton, and I look out the plane window. We see green, grassy rolling hills, with tall mountains rising in the background. We have just landed in Costa Rica.
    (*A Rain Forest Adventure,* Christine and Anton Economos, Newbridge)

L	CR	BR	P	
				TRADE BOOK MODELS
				Butterfly House, Eve Bunting
				Castle, David Macaulay (**intermediate**)
				Catch the Wind!: All About Kites, Gail Gibbons
				Eaglet's World, Evelyn White Minshull
				Fossils Tell of Long Ago, Aliki
				Mister Seahorse, Eric Carle
				My Visit to the Aquarium, Aliki
				Paddle-to-the-Sea, Holling Clancy Holling
				Pottery Place, Gail Gibbons
				Sunken Treasure, Gail Gibbons
				Sun Up, Sun Down, Gail Gibbons
				The Magic School Bus on the Ocean Floor, Joanna Cole

L	CR	BR	P	
				EDUCATIONAL BOOK MODELS
				A Rain Forest Adventure, Christine and Anton Economos (Newbridge)
				Going to the City, Marcia S. Freeman (Rand McNally, *People, Spaces, and Places*), Big Book
				_____
				_____
				_____
				_____
				_____

Fiction

Fictional stories are plot-driven. The main character has a goal to reach and conflicts to resolve. The writer creates tension through plot and through the use of tension devices, such as setbacks and pre-shadowing. A story is organized in a chronological sequence of events but may include flashbacks—scenes that took place at an earlier time.

There are only six basic plot types, but writers often use them in combinations. A story may be about a character with a goal but also feature villains trying to thwart the hero. What differs from story to story of the same plot type are the settings; motives; themes; setbacks; tension-building devices; the writer's style, tone, and voice; and most important, the characters.

Successful fiction writers create characters that their readers care about and want to succeed. The writers reveal the personality of the main characters and show how each of them changes over the course of the story. To do this, writers use the technique of description and relate what the characters say, think, and do, as well as what other characters say about them.

Fiction models for each plot type

1. Character with a problem or goal: The character solves or reaches goal.

L	CR	BR	P	TRADE BOOK MODELS
				Alexander and the Wind-Up Mouse, Leo Lionni
				Because of Winn-Dixie, Kate DiCamillo (Newbery Award) **(intermediate)**
				Berlioz the Bear, Jan Brett
				Big Al, Andrew Clements
				Catfish and Spaghetti, Marcia S. Freeman **(intermediate)**
				Corduroy, Don Freeman
				Kate's Giants, Valiska Gregory
				Miss Nelson Has a Field Day, Harry Allard and James Marshall
				Mommy Go Away!, Lynne Jonell
				Tales of a Fourth Grade Nothing, Judy Blume **(intermediate)**
				The Biggest Bear, Lynd Ward
				The Gift, Marcia S. Freeman
				Walter the Baker, Eric Carle
				_____
				_____

L	CR	BR	P	TRADE BOOK MODELS (cont.)
				_____
				_____
				_____

2. Character vs. nature: The character survives

L	CR	BR	P	TRADE BOOK MODELS
				Amos & Boris, William Steig
				Flood, Mary Calhoun
				Little House on the Prairie, Laura Ingalls Wilder
				My Side of the Mountain, Jean Craighead George **(intermediate)**
				Oonawassee Summer, Melissa Forney **(intermediate)**
				Paddle-to-the-Sea, Holling Clancy Holling
				Thunder Cake, Patricia Polacco
				Two Bad Ants, Chris Van Allsburg
				_____
				_____
				_____
				_____

3. Lost and found: The character loses and subsequently finds something. Or the character is lost, then found.

L	CR	BR	P	TRADE BOOK MODELS
				Arthur Lost and Found, Marc Brown
				Because of Winn-Dixie, Kate DiCamillo (Newbery Award) **(intermediate)**
				Blueberries for Sal, Robert McCloskey
				Finders Keepers for Franklin, Paulette Bourgeois
				Franklin Is Lost, Paulette Bourgeois
				Little Polar Bear and the Husky Pup, Hans de Beer
				Lost in the Museum, Miriam Cohen

L	CR	BR	P

TRADE BOOK MODELS (cont.)

Part-Time Dog, Jane Thayer

Stuart Little, E. B. White **(intermediate)**

Sylvester and the Magic Pebble, William Steig

The Hat, Jan Brett

The Lost and Found, Mark Teague

The Mitten, Jan Brett

The Snow Lambs, Debi Gliori

_____

_____

_____

_____

_____

4. **Good guys vs. bad guys: The good guys win (but a bad guy may survive to bedevil the good guy in a sequel).**

L	CR	BR	P

TRADE BOOK MODELS

Dominic, William Steig **(intermediate)**

James and the Giant Peach, Roald Dahl **(intermediate)**

santaKid, James Patterson

The Talking Eggs, Robert D. San Souci

_____

_____

_____

_____

5. **Mystery (or crime) and solution: The character solves mystery or crime.**

L	CR	BR	P

TRADE BOOK MODELS

Hershel and the Hanukkah Goblins, Eric Kimmel

Holes, Louis Sachar (Newbery Award) **(intermediate)**

L	CR	BR	P	
				TRADE BOOK MODELS (cont.)
				Just a Dream, Chris Van Allsburg
				Miss Nelson is Back, Harry Allard and James Marshall
				Snowmen at Night, Caralyn Buehner
				The Missing Mitten Mystery, Steven Kellogg
				The Widow's Broom, Chris Van Allsburg

6. Boy meets girl: The characters work out their problems and a happy ending ensues.

This plot type is not prevalent in children's picture books, except for fairy tales. Please make a list of your favorite fairy tales or fiction for models of this plot type.

L	CR	BR	P	
				YOUR FAVORITE MODELS

Fiction Written in the Present Tense

The present verb tense traditionally has been used by storytellers who begin their tales in the past tense, then switch to the present at a crucial moment to bring the reader right into the story.

My grandfather and I drove out to Billings Pond to fish for trout. We unloaded the canoe and piled in with all our gear. We headed straight for the beaver dam. We'd had a banner day a month ago at the start of the season. [past tense]

[And now a switch to the present tense. The storyteller wants you right with him during this exciting part.] *We're sitting in the canoe when all of a sudden here comes this moose with her calf splashing behind her. She's running right at us and my grandpa is hollering to beat the band.*

Many modern writers and many children's writers are writing entire stories in the present verb tense instead of the traditional past tense. They believe doing this engages the reader.

L	CR	BR	P	TRADE BOOK MODELS
				A Picnic in October, Eve Bunting
				Farmer's Market, Paul Brett Johnson
				Fishing Day, Andrea Davis Pinkney
				How My Library Grew: By Dinah, Martha Alexander
				Shiloh, Phyllis Reynolds Naylor (Newbery Award) **(intermediate)**
				So Far from the Sea, Eve Bunting **(intermediate)**
				The Bat Boy & His Violin, Gavin Curtis
				The Wednesday Surprise, Eve Bunting
				Train to Somewhere, Eve Bunting

Whether a piece is written in the past or present tense, if time passes, it remains a narrative. [See **Chapter 3, II. Expository, Personal Observational Expository (quasi-narrative)** for another genre that mimics narrative but is classified as expository].

Genre Skills Specific to Narrative

Storywriters have some craft techniques in their toolbox that are specific to narrative. These techniques have to do with dialogue and paragraphing conventions.

1. Dialogue Tags

Dialogue tags are little pieces of text a writer adds to help readers visualize what is going on while characters are talking. They are like the stage directions in a play.

In play format:

Wolf: *"Hello, Little Red Riding Hood."* (Motions with fingers (claws) to

Red Riding Hood to come closer to the bed).

Red Riding Hood: *"Hello, Grandmother. Oooh, how big your teeth have grown!"*

(Opens eyes wide and points to wolf's long fangs).

In fiction format:

"He's huge. Oh, I knew I could catch him, I knew it!" **Kerry cried as she carefully let more line out.**
    (*Catfish and Spaghetti*, Marcia S. Freeman)

L	CR	BR	P	TRADE BOOK MODELS
				Berlioz the Bear, Jan Brett
				Catfish and Spaghetti, Marcia S. Freeman **(intermediate)**
				Flood, Mary Calhoun
				Galimoto, Karen Lynn Williams
				Happy Birthday, Moon, Frank Asch
				James and the Giant Peach, Roald Dahl
				Last Summer with Maizon, Jacqueline Woodson **(intermediate)**
				Oonawassee Summer, Melissa Forney **(intermediate)**
				Soup, Robert Newton Peck **(intermediate)**
				Stellaluna, Janell Cannon
				The Slippery Slope, Lemony Snicket **(intermediate)**
				The Watsons Go to Birmingham—1963, Christopher Paul Curtis (Newbery Award) **(intermediate)**
				Zelda and Ivy and the Boy Next Door, Laura McGee Kvasnosky
				_____
				_____
				_____
				_____
				_____

2. Paragraphing Narratives

To help readers keep track of the time, place, and characters in their stories, writers break up their narratives into paragraphs that show changes of *time, place, action,* and *speaker.* They use cue words at the start of a paragraph that tell the reader when and where they are. Young writers should be taught to revise their drafts by replacing *and thens* and *thens* with cue words or transitions.

Paragraphing is also used to help readers keep track of who is talking during dialogue. Storywriters begin a new paragraph each time the speaker changes. They place quotation marks around words coming directly out of a character's mouth so the reader knows those words are dialogue.

> In modern publishing, new paragraphs in stories are indicated by indenting the first line several character spaces. But in expository text, new paragraphs are indicated by a line-and-a-half spacing between paragraphs. This is a byproduct of the Computer Age. Notice when you use a word processing program and you press ENTER to move to a new paragraph, that the default style is a line-and-a-half space after each paragraph. One exception is newspaper text where space constraints do not allow publishers to give up that extra half-line. Instead, the first lines of newspaper paragraphs are indented about two character spaces.

Time transitions.

Time cues or **transitions** include words and phrases such as *Later, Suddenly, After that, The next morning, During the storm, When they came home,* and many more. Students should make and keep lists of the time transitions they find in their story readings. They should refer to their lists when they write their own stories.

The next day it snowed so heavily that it was impossible to open the door. The snow kept falling for five or six days, and the young lady stayed on, wondering all the while how she could repay the old couple for their kindness toward her.
   (*The Crane's Gift,* Steve and Megumi Biddle)

L	CR	BR	P	
				TRADE BOOK MODELS
				Alexander and the Wind-Up Mouse, Leo Lionni
				Birthday Presents, Cynthia Rylant
				Castle, David Macaulay **(intermediate)**
				Catfish and Spaghetti, Marcia S. Freeman **(intermediate)**
				Froggy Bakes a Cake, Jonathan London

L	CR	BR	P	TRADE BOOK MODELS (cont.)
				Happy Birthday, Moon, Frank Asch
				Pottery Place, Gail Gibbons
				Sylvester and the Magic Pebble, William Steig
				Tales of a Fourth Grade Nothing, Judy Blume (**intermediate**)
				The Crane's Gift, Steve and Megumi Biddle
				The Gift, Marcia S. Freeman
				The Other Side, Jacqueline Woodson
				The Relatives Came, Cynthia Rylant

_____

_____

_____

_____

Place transitions.

Place-cues or **transitions** include words and phrases such as *Under the porch, Across the yard, Inside the house, Meanwhile back at the ranch, At the window,* and the like.

An example:

Juan jumped out of bed and headed to the kitchen. He padded softly down the hall, carefully closing the door behind him as he went into the kitchen.

***At the window,** his mama was clipping laundry to the pulley clothesline that stretched from their window across the courtyard to the wall of the apartment opposite. She motioned him to the table with her head, her mouth filled with extra clothespins.*

***Juan sat at the table** and fiddled with his spoon and bowl. Sighing, he reached for the serving bowl at the center of the table and pulled it closer to his bowl...*

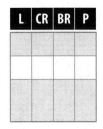

L	CR	BR	P	TRADE BOOK MODELS
				Blueberries for Sal, Robert McCloskey
				Castle, David Macaulay (**intermediate**)
				Catfish and Spaghetti, Marcia S. Freeman (**intermediate**)

L	CR	BR	P	

TRADE BOOK MODELS (cont.)

Pottery Place, Gail Gibbons

Sylvester and the Magic Pebble, William Steig

The Crane's Gift, Steve and Megumi Biddle

The Reptile Room, Lemony Snicket **(intermediate)**

Changes in action.

Writers do not use cue words to indicate a **change in action**. They simply start a new paragraph to cue the reader that there has been a change. From the action description, the reader can generally infer where the action is occurring.

An example:

Juan **wolfed down his breakfast**, barely tasting the toast or cereal. He wondered how he could get to school before Kyle showed up in the playground. He gulped his milk and made a dash for his room.

Throwing on his clothes, he kicked his pajamas under the bed. He made a fast job of making his bed, flinging the blanket over his pillow and running a hand quickly over it all to smooth it out. He grabbed his book bag and hurried back to the kitchen to get his lunch.

The subway station was packed as **he made his way to the uptown end of the station...**

All narratives use paragraphing such as this to show changes of action. Rather than list any such books here, you and your students are invited to find favorites from your classroom collections.

L	CR	BR	P	

YOUR FAVORITE MODELS

Change in speaker.

Most dialogue is divided between two or more speakers, and every time the speaker changes, writers begin a new paragraph. Because of this convention, in conversations between just two characters, the writer does not always need to add *"said character x"* to indicate who has spoken. The reader understands that the two speakers alternate and that, unless otherwise indicated, a new paragraph means the speaker has changed.

If, however, a character is making an extended speech that needs to be divided into paragraphs, then the writer would add enough dialogue tags to keep the reader from getting confused when the speaker changes. A good writer does not want his readers to be confused.

Example of regular dialogue with paragraphing to show change of speaker. Notice the dialogue tags as well.

"I'm hungry!" the Spider announced suddenly, staring hard at James.

"I'm famished!" the Old-Green-Grasshopper said.

"So am I!" the Ladybug cried.

The Centipede sat up a little straighter on the sofa. "Everyone's famished!" he said. "We need food."
    (*James and the Giant Peach*, Roald Dahl)

Almost all fiction books have dialogue and dialogue tags, and are thus good models of paragraphing for change of speaker. Rather than list any such books here, you and your students are invited to find favorites from your classroom collections.

L	CR	BR	P	YOUR FAVORITE MODELS
				_____
				_____
				_____
				_____
				_____

Expository

Expository books fall into many categories and genres. They may be single-concept books about such things as color, shape, shadows, or light. They may be descriptive or informational texts presented in poetry or prose. They may be how-to books. They may describe processes such as life cycles of living things and manufacturing, or systems such as the rain cycle and milk production from cow to cup. They may present information through comparison, problem and solution, or cause-and-effect. They may be essays of opinion or persuasion. They may be art- or photo-illustrated. What they are *not* are stories.

Expository text is organized by clumping related information (or ideas and concepts) or by ordering a sequence of steps. The table of contents reveals this clumping or the step sequence. Point that out to your students when you read from these books. Point out also that authors can, and usually do, put bits of expository text in a story.

Informational Text

Well-written expository **informational text** is engaging. Its writers achieve this in a number of ways. They use creative hooks and ending techniques. They employ vivid imagery (see **Chapter 2, Description: Skills for Creating Imagery**). They talk directly to their readers using the pronouns *you, we, I,* and *us.* They embed definitions of content words in the text so their readers do not have to constantly flip back and forth to the glossary. They present the information in a logically organized form so their readers can easily follow the text.

> Science-standards-based, guided reading books, which are informational texts, are especially useful in teaching ELL students to read. These students' background experiences are considerably more likely to be activated when the topic is weather, animals, plants, water, or rocks as opposed to magic snowflakes or talking trains. Informational text about science is almost always culturally neutral.

Informational Text Structure

Expository writing is most often presented in clumps of related information or ideas. To show how the bits of information relate to each other, writers use a variety of text structures within their piece. These could include description, contrast, comparison, main idea and support, main idea and multiple examples, definition, step order, and cause-and-effect.

The bibliographies that follow refer both to whole books that are based on identified organization schemes, as well as those that contain paragraphs of various text structures.

Main idea (and perhaps subtopics) with supporting details.

Writers know that their readers expect details in support of their **main ideas.** If a writer says, *"Whales are large mammals,"* readers expect to hear about the size of whales and their mammalian attributes. Writers provide supporting details of facts, description, numbers, comparisons, authoritative quotes, anecdotes, and graphics to prove their main ideas.

L	CR	BR	P	
				TRADE BOOK MODELS
				Animal Dads, Sneed B. Collard III
				Eating the Alphabet, Lois Elhert
				Let's Go Home: The Wonderful Things About a House, Cynthia Rylant
				The Important Book, Margaret Wise Brown
				So You Want to Be President?, Judith St. George (Caldecott Award)
				Twilight Comes Twice, Ralph Fletcher

L	CR	BR	P	
				EDUCATIONAL BOOK MODELS
				As Big As a Whale, Melvin Berger (Newbridge, *Ranger Rick*) Big Book
				Animal Covers, Luana K. Mitten and Mary Wagner (Rourke, *Readers for Writers*)
				Conquering Mount Everest, Jackie Glassman (Benchmark, *Navigators*)
				From Farms to You, Paul McEvoy (Newbridge, *Go Facts*)
				Getting Dinner, Jennifer Blizin Gillis (Rourke, *Readers for Writers*)
				Life in America's First Cities, Sally Senzell Isaacs (Heinneman Library)
				People and the Sea, Sharon Dalgleish and Garda Turner (Newbridge, *Go Facts*)
				Planes, Ian Rohr (Newbridge, *Go Facts*)
				Sea Life, Katy Pike and Garda Turner (Newbridge, *Go Facts*)
				Simple Machines, Melvin Berger (Newbridge, *Early Science*), Big Book
				Sorting It All Out, Luana K. Mitten and Mary Wagner (Rourke, *Readers for Writers*)
				The Rain Forest, Melvin Berger (Newbridge, *Ranger Rick*), Big Book
				Trains, Ian Rohr (Newbridge, *Go Facts*)

L	CR	BR	P	EDUCATIONAL BOOK MODELS (cont.)
				Wetlands, Marcia S. Freeman (Newbridge, *Early Science*), Big Book
				What Plant is This?, Marcia S. Freeman (Rourke, *Readers for Writers*), Big Book
				You Are a Scientist, Marcia S. Freeman (Rourke, *Readers for Writers*), Big Book
				_____
				_____
				_____
				_____
				_____

Main idea with many examples.

Some informational writing explores one subject and all the varieties of that subject, such as butterflies and the kinds of butterflies, or rivers and the major rivers found in North America.

L	CR	BR	P	TRADE BOOK MODELS
				Boat Book, Gail Gibbons
				How a House is Built, Gail Gibbons
				Leaf Jumpers, Carole Gerber
				So You Want to Be President?, Judith St. George (Caldecott Award)
				Spiders, Gail Gibbons
				The Underwater Alphabet Book, Jerry Pallotta
				Tool Book, Gail Gibbons
				Whales, Gail Gibbons
				What Daddies Do Best, Laura Joffe Numeroff
				What Mommies Do Best, Laura Joffe Numeroff

L	CR	BR	P	EDUCATIONAL BOOK MODELS
				Animals in Hiding, Melvin Berger (Newbridge, *Early Science*), Big Book
				At the Pond, Marcia S. Freeman (Rourke, *Readers for Writers*)

L	CR	BR	P

EDUCATIONAL BOOK MODELS (cont.)

Dinosaurs, Melvin Berger (Newbridge, *Early Science*), Big Book

It's a Good Thing There Are Insects, Allan Fowler (Children's Press), Big Book

Sticky Stuff, Luana K. Mitten and Mary Wagner (Rourke, *Readers for Writers*)

Where Do You Live?, Marcia S. Freeman (Rand McNally, *People, Spaces, and Places*), Big Book

Young Geographers, Marcia S. Freeman (Rand McNally, *People, Spaces, and Places*), Big Book

Directions, life cycles, procedures, and process description.

Directions, or **descriptions of procedures or processes**, are presented as a list or in running text. When it is list-like, the writer usually uses imperative verbs. List-like text is conventionally bulleted or numbered.

a. Open the seed package.

b. Dig a row of holes in the soil about two inches deep.

c. Place one seed in each hole.

d. Water every day…etc.

Running text makes use of transitions such as *after that, first, next, when,* and *finally* to establish step order.

If you want to build a birdhouse, you will need plywood, small nails, a hammer, a saw, and a plan. **First,** *check your plan to find out how much plywood you need.* **Then,** *using the plan, make pattern pieces from paper and lay them on the plywood. Trace around them.* **Next,** *saw around each pattern piece, cutting it from the plywood…*

Narrative writing, including fiction, can contain passages of process description, too. I have included some examples in the list below.

L	CR	BR	P	TRADE BOOK MODELS
				Cactus Hotel, Brenda Z. Guiberson
				Cecily Cicada, Kita Helmetag Murdock
				Charlie Needs a Cloak, Tomie dePaola
				Chicken Soup with Rice: A Book of Months, Maurice Sendak
				How Do Apples Grow?, Betsy Maestro
				Land of the Dark, Land of the Light: The Arctic National Wildlife Refuge, Karen Pandell
				Outside and Inside Sharks, Sandra Markle
				Pancakes, Pancakes!, Eric Carle
				Pottery Place, Gail Gibbons
				Seal Pup Grows Up: The Story of a Harbor Seal, Kathleen Weidner Zoehfeld
				Snowballs, Lois Ehlert
				Sun Up, Sun Down, Gail Gibbons
				The Biggest, Best Snowman, Margery Cuyler
				The Everglades, Jean Craighead George
				The Grouchy Ladybug, Eric Carle
				The Honey Makers, Gail Gibbons
				The Snowman, Raymond Briggs
				The Pumpkin Book, Gail Gibbons
				The Tiny Seed, Eric Carle
				The Tortilla Factory, Gary Paulsen
				The Very Hungry Caterpillar, Eric Carle
				Vote!, Eileen Christelow

L	CR	BR	P	EDUCATIONAL BOOK MODELS
				Animal Lives, Marcia S. Freeman (Rourke, *Readers for Writers*), Big Book
				Back to the Sea, Patty Whitehouse (Rourke, *Readers for Writers*)
				Frogs and Toads and Tadpoles, Too!, Allan Fowler (Children's Press), Big Book
				From Farms to You, Paul McEvoy (Newbridge, *Go Facts*)

L	CR	BR	P

EDUCATIONAL BOOK MODELS (cont.)

From the Factory, Nancy White (Newbridge, *Early Social Studies*), Big Book

Fungi, Mary Kay Carson (Newbridge, *Ranger Rick*), Big Book

Going to the City, Marcia S. Freeman (Rand McNally, *People, Spaces, and Places*), Big Book

Growing a Kitchen Garden, Natalie Lunis (Benchmark, *Navigators*)

Insects, Katy Pike (Newbridge, *Go Facts*)

Leaping Frogs, Melvin Berger (Newbridge, *Early Science*), Big Book

Let's Experiment, Natalie Lunis and Nancy White (Newbridge, *Thinking Like a Scientist*), Big Book

Life Cycle of a Dog, Angela Royston (Heinemann Library)

Life Cycle of a Monarch Butterfly, Jennifer Blizin Gillis (Rourke, *Readers for Writers*)

Life in America's First Cities, Sally Senzell Isaacs (Heinemann Library)

Make Mine Ice Cream, Melvin Berger (Newbridge, *Early Science*), Big Book

Popcorn Science, Natalie Lunis and Nancy White (Newbridge, *Thinking Like a Scientist*), Big Book

The Seasons of the Year, Marcia S. Freeman (Rourke, *Readers for Writers*), Big Book

Comparison.

Comparison is all about presenting similarities and differences. It is an important **critical thinking skill**. Robert Marzano's research (2003) found that of all the instructional strategies that positively affect student achievement, helping students *identify similarities and differences* (in other words, making comparisons) had the largest average effect on achievement.

Comparison lies at the heart of analytical thinking. Writing comparison papers is a task students are called upon to do throughout their school careers. To do it successfully, they need to hear and see models of comparison often. (See also **Chapter 2: Description, Skills for Creating Imagery, Literary Devices for Comparisons**).

Authors use a text structure of paired sentences or paired paragraphs to compare two things. Some whole books are based on a comparison text structure. The first list below is of books that exhibit sentences and paragraphs of comparison text structure. The second list contains books organized entirely by a comparison text structure.

Paired sentences:

On Friday nights, I like to go to bed early and get up real early. But my friend, Mike, likes to stay up as late as he can and sleep away Saturday morning.

Paired paragraphs:

"We will take our berries home and can them," said her mother. Then we will have food for winter." Sal's mother walked slowly through the bushes, picking blueberries as she went and putting them in her pail...."

On the other side of Blueberry Hill, Little Bear came with his mother to eat blueberries. "Little Bear," she said, "eat lots of berries and grow big and fat. We must store up food for the long, cold winter."
   (Blueberries for Sal, Robert McCloskey)

Models of books containing comparison text structures

L	CR	BR	P	TRADE BOOK MODELS
				Big Tracks, Little Tracks, Millicent E. Selsam
				Check It Out!: The Book About Libraries, Gail Gibbons
				It's Winter, Linda Glaser
				Outside and Inside Sharks, Sandra Markle
				Sharks, Seymour Simon
				So You Want to Be President?, Judith St. George (Caldecott Award)
				Subway Sonata, Patricia Lakin
				Through Grandpa's Eyes, Patricia MacLachlan
				Twilight Comes Twice, Ralph Fletcher
				The Underwater Alphabet Book, Jerry Pallotta

L	CR	BR	P	EDUCATIONAL BOOK MODELS
				Animal Lives, Marcia S. Freeman (Rourke, *Readers for Writers*), Big Book
				Birds, Paul McEvoy (Newbridge, *Go Facts*)
				Everything Under the Sun, Marcia S. Freeman (Rourke, *Readers for Writers*), Big Book
				Flowers, Paul McEvoy (Newbridge, *Go Facts*)
				Let's Look at Rocks, Luana K. Mitten and Mary Wagner (Rourke, *Readers for Writers*)
				Polar Regions, Alison Ballance (Dominie Press)
				Short, Tall, Big or Small?, Kari Jenson Gold (Newbridge, *Early Math*)
				Sorting It All Out, Luana K. Mitten and Mary Wagner (Rourke, *Readers for Writers*)
				Trains, Ian Rohr (Newbridge, *Go Facts*)
				What Do We Pay For?, Marilyn J. Salomon (Newbridge, *Early Social Studies*), Big Book
				What Plant is This?, Marcia S. Freeman (Rourke, *Readers for Writers*), Big Book
				What is Hot? What is Not?, Luana K. Mitten and Mary Wagner (Rourke, *Readers for Writers*)

_____

_____

_____

_____

_____

Models of books entirely organized by comparison

L	CR	BR	P	TRADE BOOK MODELS
				A Turkey for Thanksgiving, Eve Bunting
				Big Tracks, Little Tracks, Millicent E. Selsam
				Blueberries for Sal, Robert McCloskey
				Gert & Frieda, Anita Riggio
				Henry Hikes to Fitchburg, D.B. Johnson
				Inside Mouse, Outside Mouse, Lindsay Barrett George

L	CR	BR	P

TRADE BOOK MODELS (cont.)

Nana Upstairs & Nana Downstairs, Tomie De Paolo

Super-Completely and Totally the Messiest, Judith Viorst

The Napping House Wakes Up, Audrey Wood

The Quiltmaker's Gift, Jeff Brumbeau

Town Mouse, Country Mouse, Jan Brett

Twilight Comes Twice, Ralph Fletcher

What Daddies Do Best, Laura Joffe Numeroff

What Mommies Do Best, Laura Joffe Numeroff

What Was I Scared Of?, Dr. Seuss

_____

_____

_____

_____

_____

Definition.

Non-fiction writers often present information through **definition**, devoting one or several sentences to defining a word or concept.

The lizard's disguise is simple camouflage. Camouflage is an animal's way of using its color to blend into its surroundings.
   (*Reptiles*, Lynn Stone, Rourke)

L	CR	BR	P

EDUCATIONAL BOOK MODELS

Acids and Bases, Lisa Benjamin (Newbridge, *Ranger Rick*), Big Book

Backyard Scientist, Natalie Lunis (Newbridge, *Thinking Like a Scientist*), Big Book

Being a Scientist, Natalie Lunis and Nancy White (Newbridge, *Thinking Like a Scientist*), Big Book

Coast to Coast, Marcia S. Freeman (Rand McNally, *People, Spaces, and Places*), Big Book

Fungi, Mary Kay Carson (Newbridge, *Ranger Rick*), Big Book

Everything Under the Sun, Marcia S. Freeman (Rourke, *Readers for Writers*), Big Book

L	CR	BR	P	EDUCATIONAL BOOK MODELS (cont.)

Getting Ready to Race, Susan Ring (Newbridge, *Discovery Links*)

Patterns in Nature, Jennifer Blizin Gillis (Rourke, *Readers for Writers*)

Reptiles, Lynn M. Stone (Rourke, *Animals in Disguise*)

Sea Anemones, Lynn Stone (Rourke, *Science Under the Sea*)

Science Tools, J.A. Randolph (Newbridge, *Early Science*), Big Book

Sea Life, Katy Pike and Garda Turner (Newbridge, *Go Facts*)

Shorebirds, Melissa Stewart (Newbridge, *Ranger Rick*), Big Book

Trains, Ian Rohr (Newbridge, *Go Facts*)

The Web of Life, Melvin Berger (Newbridge, *Ranger Rick*), Big Book

The World of Dinosaurs, Melvin Berger (Newbridge, *Early Science*), Big Book

Why Polar Bears Like Snow…And Flamingos Don't, Nancy White (Benchmark, *Navigators*)

Young Geographers, Marcia S. Freeman (Rand McNally, *People, Spaces, and Places*), Big Book

_____

_____

_____

_____

Cause and Effect.

As writers present information, they often must show readers the relationship of one thing to another. Sometimes they show that one thing causes another (a **causal relationship**): *When it rains, the irrigation ditches fill up.*

L	CR	BR	P	TRADE BOOK MODELS

Dolphins, Tammy Everts and Bobbie Kalman

If You Give a Pig a Pancake, Laura Joffe Numeroff

L	CR	BR	P

TRADE BOOK MODELS (cont.)

If You Take a Mouse to School, Laura Joffe Numeroff

If You Give a Mouse a Cookie, Laura Joffe Numeroff

If You Give a Moose a Muffin, Laura Joffe Numeroff

Manatee: On Location, Kathy Darling

Outside and Inside Sharks, Sandra Markle

The Everglades, Jean Craighead George

The Mitten, Jan Brett

L	CR	BR	P

EDUCATIONAL BOOK MODELS

A Rain Forest Adventure, Christine and Anton Economos (Newbridge, *Discovery Links*)

A World of Change, Natalie Lunis and Nancy White (Newbridge, *Thinking Like a Scientist*), Big Book

Flowers, Paul McEvoy (Newbridge, *Go Facts*)

Investigating Rocks, Natalie Lunis and Nancy White (Newbridge, *Thinking Like a Scientist*), Big Book

It's Best to Leave a Snake Alone, Allan Fowler (Children's Press), Big Book

Oceans, Katy Pike and Maureen O'Keefe (Newbridge, *Go Facts*)

Sea Life, Katy Pike and Garda Turner (Newbridge, *Go Facts*)

Smart, Clean Pigs, Allan Fowler (Children's Press), Big Book

Woolly Sheep and Hungry Goats, Allan Fowler (Children's Press), Big Book

Why Polar Bears Like Snow…And Flamingos Don't, Nancy White (Benchmark, *Navigators*)

Personal Expository

Some children's books are written in a personal-expository mode, in the first person, and most often in a child's voice. They tell about the author-child's feelings and knowledge. As such, they make good models for the kind of writing that primary students do naturally.

Young writers in the primary grades write to tell us what they know, what they did, and what they feel:

Bo is my dog and he acts like a puppy. I love my dog.
   (Kindergarten)

I went to my Nana's and we made cookies. I made square cookies with a cutter. Nana puts molasses in cookies.
   (First-grader)

Last June I got twin baby sisters. The worst thing is that there are two of them. They need two cribs. And two highchairs. And two of everything.
   (*Twinnies*, Eve Bunting)

L	CR	BR	P	TRADE BOOK MODELS
				A. Lincoln and Me, Louise Borden
				Fly Away Home, Eve Bunting
				I Loved You Before You Were Born, Anne Bowen
				I Used To Be the Baby, Robin Ballard
				Like a Windy Day, Frank and Devin Asch
				My Daddy and Me, Jerry Spinelli
				My Little Brother, David McPhail
				The Pain and the Great One, Judy Blume
				Twinnies, Eve Bunting
				When I Get Bigger, Mercer Mayer
				When I Was Young in the Mountains, Cynthia Rylant
				While You Are Away, Eileen Spinelli

Personal Observational Expository (quasi-narrative)

Have you ever come across a children's picture book that you aren't sure of whether it is a story or not? It reads something like a personal narrative, but it is written in the present tense. It may be written in the first person and in a child's voice. The author is describing something she observes or does. The writing is highly descriptive and may evoke strong feelings. The setting plays an important part in the piece. **The writing is most often subject-oriented.** The text may look something like this:

In the summer my grandmother and I go fishing. She packs a big picnic while I gather the fishing equipment. We walk to the river to find our favorite place. Sometimes we catch fish and sometimes we don't. We don't care.

This kind of writing defies easy definition or categorizing. For example, you could say this sample text is a personal expository piece about fishing with my grandmother. Or, you could call it an observational descriptive piece. I call it **quasi-narrative personal observational expository**, which I admit is quite a mouthful. This just goes to show that writers may do anything they like!

By any name, this peculiar genre is the perfect model for the way kindergarteners and first-graders talk about their experiences before they master time sequencing. They tell of their weekend, writing about the most important thing first, then the next thing they remember, and so forth.

I went to my uncle's. He took me fishing. We watched TV. We ate watermelon and spit out the seeds. My uncle is fun.
   (student writing)

Such writing is not truly a narrative as there is no definitive time sequence, nor any point or plot for that matter. The time sequence is not really important to the young writer, who just wants to tell us the highlights of what happened.

L	CR	BR	P	TRADE BOOK MODELS
				Africa Dream, Eloise Greenfield
				Canoe Days, Gary Paulsen
				Eloise, Kay Thompson
				Let's Go Home: The Wonderful Things About a House, Cynthia Rylant
				My Visit to the Dinosaurs, Aliki

L	CR	BR	P

EDUCATIONAL BOOK MODELS

Clay Hernandez: A Mexican American, Diane Hoyt-Goldsmith (Newbridge)

_____

_____

_____

_____

_____

Persuasion

Writers of persuasive text present an opinion or state their position on an issue and then go on to support it with facts and statistics, logical arguments, comparisons, authoritative quotes, anecdotes, and the like.

Children's books do not commonly exemplify persuasive writing craft. A few do, and you're invited to find more.

L	CR	BR	P

TRADE BOOK MODELS

Animals Should Definitely Not Wear Clothing, Judi Barrett

Dear Children of the Earth, Schim Schimmel

Earrings!, Judith Viorst

Hey! Get Off Our Train, John Burningham

The Great Kapok Tree: A Tale of the Amazon Rain Forest, Lynne Cherry

Where Once There Was a Wood, Denise Fleming

L	CR	BR	P

EDUCATIONAL BOOK MODELS

Should There Be Zoos?, Tony Stead with students (Mondo Big Book)

_____

_____

_____

_____

_____

Friendly Letters

Friendly letters may be narrative, expository, or a mixture of both.

Narrative - When a letter is narrative in nature, its writer tells of events, putting them in chronological order and writing them in the past tense.

Dear Nana,
Last week my class went to the zoo. I carried the mammal guidebook you gave me for my birthday. When we got to the zoo, we went to the primate house first. (That is where the monkeys and apes are). We ate lunch right across from the seals. After lunch, my friend Shasta threw up when we were in the reptile house. She was afraid of the lizards. After that, we went into the aviary. Nothing was scary there. We had fun.

Love, Kate

Expository - When a letter is purely expository in nature, its writer clumps related facts or ideas and uses present-tense verbs.

Dear Nana,
I love the mammal guidebook you sent to me for my birthday. So far I have seen 12 different mammals that are in the book. My favorite ones are rodents. You can find them everywhere. Did you know rodents all have the same kind of teeth? Two big front ones, like a beaver's or a gerbil's. Thank you again for the book,

Love, Kate

Friendly letter conventions, while not written in stone, include salutation and closing formats. Postcards work the same way, though writers often leave off the salutation to have more writing space.

With the advent of e-mail and cellular phones, friendly letters are somewhat becoming a thing of the past—unfortunately, along with clear, grammatical, and well-organized writing. Nonetheless, in spite of this media change, lessons in and practice with writing friendly letters is still relevant.

L	CR	BR	P

TRADE BOOK MODELS

Click, Clack, Moo: Cows That Type, Doreen Cronin

Dear Mr. Blueberry, Simon James

Dear Mrs. LaRue: Letters from Obedience School, Mark Teague

Dear Peter Rabbit, Alma Flor Ada

Detective LaRue, Mark Teague

L	CR	BR	P

TRADE BOOK MODELS (cont.)

The Armadillo from Amarillo, Lynne Cherry **(intermediate)**

The Gardener, Sarah Stewart

The Jolly Postman, Janet and Allan Ahlberg

With Love, Little Red Hen, Alma Flor Ada

Yours Truly, Goldilocks, Alma Flor Ada

L	CR	BR	P

EDUCATIONAL BOOK MODELS

Dear Grandma, Avelyn Davidson (Shortland Publications, *Storyteller*)

_____

_____

_____

_____

Educational Publishers

Benchmark Education Company: www.benchmarkeducation.com

Children's Press: www.childrenspress.com

Creative Teacher's Press, Inc.: www.creativeteaching.com

Dominie Press: www.dominie.com

Heinemann Library: www.heinemannlibrary.com

Lerner Publishing Group: www.lernerbooks.com

Newbridge Educational Publishing: www.newbridgeonline.com

Raintree: www.raintreelibrary.com

Rand McNally & Company: www.randmcnally.com

Rigby: www.rigby.com

Rourke Classroom Resources: www.rourkeclassroom.com

Rourke Publishing: www.rourkepublishing.com

Shortland Publications/The Wright Group: www.wrightgroup.com

Professional Books

Anderson-McElveen, Susan and Connie Campbell Dierking. *Literature Models to Teach Expository Writing*. Gainesville, FL: Maupin House, 2001.

Baur, Marion Dane. *What's Your Story?* NY: Clarion Books, 1992.

Forney, Melissa. *Razzle Dazzle Writing: Achieving Success Through 50 Target Skills*. Gainesville, FL: Maupin House, 2001.

Freeman, Marcia S. *Building a Writing Community: A Practical Guide.* Gainesville, FL: Maupin House, 1995.

Freeman, Marcia S. *CraftPlus: Writing Program and Staff Development Resource.* Gainesville, FL: Maupin House, 1998.

Freeman, Marcia S. *Teaching the Youngest Writers: A Practical Guide.* Gainesville, FL: Maupin House, 1998.

Hall, Susan. *Using Picture Storybooks to Teach Literary Devices.* Phoenix, AZ: Oryx Press, 1990.

Marzano, Robert. *What Works in Schools: Translating Research into Action.* Alexandria, VA: Association for Supervision and Curriculum Development, 2003.

Provost, Gary. *100 Ways To Improve Your Writing.* New York, NY: New American Library, 1985.

Schrecengost, Maity. *Writing Whizardry: 60 Mini-Lessons to Teach Elaboration and Writer's Craft.* Gainesville, FL: Maupin House, 2001.

Scholes, Robert. *The Rise and Fall of English: Reconstructing English as a Discipline.* New Haven, CT: Yale University Press, 1998.

Shanahan, T. "Reading-writing Relationships, Thematic Units, Inquiry Learning. In Pursuit of Effective Integrated Literacy Instruction," *Reading Teacher* 51:1 (1997): 12-19.

Zinsser, William, ed. *Inventing the Truth: The Art and Craft of Memoir.* Boston: Houghton Mifflin Co., 1987.

Index of Literature Cited

Target Skills Cross-Index
and
Blank Target Skills Templates

TITLE and AUTHOR

TITLE and AUTHOR	DESCRIPTION						ORGANIZATION				INFORMATIONAL TEXT STRUCTURE						LITERARY COMPOSING							
	STRONG VERBS	ATTRIBUTE ADJECTIVES	COMPARISONS	PERSONIFICATION	ONOMATOPOEIA	SPECIFICITY	BEGINNINGS	ENDINGS	TIME TRANSITIONS	PLACE TRANSITIONS	MAIN IDEA	MAIN IDEA WITH EXAMPLES	STEP SEQUENCING WITH SUPPORTING DETAILS	COMPARISON	DEFINITION	CAUSE and EFFECT	ALLITERATION	CONTRAST	EMBEDDED DEFINITION	CLUES TO PROVIDE INFERENCE	REPETITION	SENTENCE VARIATION	DIALOGUE TAGS	VOICE
A Bird's-Eye View, Marcia S. Freeman								✓																
A Butterfly is Born, Melvin Berger								✓		✓														
A Day, Robin Nelson								✓																
A Is For Abigail, Lynn Cheney								✓																
A Katydid's Life, Nic Bishop								✓		✓										✓				
A Picture Book of Davy Crockett, David Adler								✓																
A Picture Book of Lewis and Clark, David A. Adler				✓			✓																	
A Pinky is a Baby Mouse: And Other Baby Animal Names, Pam Muñoz Ryan			✓															✓						✓
A Rain Forest Adventure, Christine and Anton Economos							✓	✓									✓							
A Turkey for Thanksgiving, Eve Bunting								✓								✓								
A World of Change, Natalie Lunis and Nancy White								✓								✓	✓							
A. Lincoln and Me, Louise Borden					✓																			
Acids and Bases, Lisa Benjamin																						✓		✓
Africa Dream, Eloise Greenfield																							✓	

Title, Author	1	2	3	4	5	6	7	8	9	10	11	12	13	14	15	16	17	18	19
Air Around Us, Luana K. Mitten and Mary Wagner						✓									✓				
Alexander and the Wind-Up Mouse, Leo Lionni							✓												
Alexander, Who's Not (Do you hear me? I mean it!) Going to Move, Judith Viorst						✓													
All About Wood, Jennifer Prescott						✓	✓												
Amazing Crickets, Daniel Jacobs																✓		✓	
Amazing Rain Forest, Ted O'Hare						✓										✓		✓	
Amelia and Eleanor Go For a Ride, Pam Muñoz Ryan						✓													
America: A Patriotic Primer, Lynn Cheney							✓												
Among the Flowers, David M. Schwartz		✓														✓		✓	
Amos & Boris, William Steig					✓										✓				
An Octopus Is Amazing, Patricia Lauber						✓										✓		✓	
Animal Covers, Luana K. Mitten and Mary Wagner							✓		✓										✓
Animal Dads, Sneed B. Collard III							✓									✓			✓
Animal Homes, Susan Hartley and Shane Armstrong															✓				
Animal Lives, Marcia S. Freeman	✓						✓			✓	✓							✓	
Animals and Their Babies, Melvin Berger						✓													
Animals and Their Colors, Stephanie Maze							✓												
Animals in Hiding, Melvin Berger			✓							✓							✓		
Ant Cities, Arthur Dorros					✓		✓												
Apples to Oregon, Deborah Hopkinson and Nancy Carpenter							✓												
Apples, Gail Gibbons						✓													
Are You a Snail?, Judy Allen																			✓

TITLE and AUTHOR

Title and Author	DESCRIPTION					ORGANIZATION		INFORMATIONAL TEXT STRUCTURE							LITERARY COMPOSING									
	STRONG VERBS	ATTRIBUTE ADJECTIVES	COMPARISONS	PERSONIFICATION	ONOMATOPOEIA	SPECIFICITY	BEGINNINGS	ENDINGS	TIME TRANSITIONS	PLACE TRANSITIONS	MAIN IDEA	MAIN IDEA WITH EXAMPLES	STEP SEQUENCING WITH SUPPORTING DETAILS	COMPARISON	DEFINITION	CAUSE and EFFECT	ALLITERATION	CONTRAST	EMBEDDED DEFINITION	CLUES TO PROVIDE INFERENCE	REPETITION	SENTENCE VARIATION	DIALOGUE TAGS	VOICE
Around the Pond: Who's Been Here?, Lindsay Barrett George			✓							✓											✓			
As Big As a Whale, Melvin Berger			✓	✓				✓												✓				✓
As: A Surfeit of Similes, Norton Juster				✓	✓							✓												
At Play in the Community, Judy Nayer								✓																
At the Farm, David M. Schwartz						✓		✓										✓			✓			
At the Pond, Marcia S. Freeman								✓						✓										
At Work, Margaret Mooney										✓											✓			
Baby Whales Drink Milk, Barbara Juster Esbensen							✓	✓																
Back to the Sea, Patty Whitehouse										✓					✓									
Backstage, Marcie Bovetz								✓																
Backyard Scientist, Natalie Lunis										✓						✓								
Badger's Parting Gifts, Susan Varley								✓																
Bats!: Strange and Wonderful, Laurence Pringle																								✓
Bats, Gail Gibbons								✓																

Title																						
Bean, David M. Schwartz	✓																					
Because of Winn-Dixie, Kate DiCamillo		✓	✓																✓	✓	✓	
Bees and Wasps, David Cutts			✓	✓									✓		✓					
Being a Scientist, Natalie Lunis and Nancy White			✓					✓											
Berlioz the Bear, Jan Brett		✓	✓															✓		✓
Bicycles, Morgan Hughes			✓																
Big Al, Andrew Clements									✓		✓										✓
Big Anthony and the Magic Ring, Tomie dePaola		✓						✓											
Big Panda, Little Panda, Joan Stimson			✓																
Big Tracks, Little Tracks, Millicent E. Selsam						✓													
Bigmama's, Donald Crews		✓																	
Billy's Picture, Margaret and HA Rey		✓					✓												
Birds, Paul McEvoy		✓	✓			✓													
Birthday Presents, Cynthia Rylant					✓														
Blood, Fay Robinson	✓		✓																
Blueberries for Sal, Robert McCloskey				✓			✓												
Boas, Ted O'Hare															✓				
Boat Book, Gail Gibbons																			
Boo to a Goose, Mem Fox	✓																		✓
Brave Irene, William Steig	✓	✓	✓																✓			✓
Brown Bear, Brown Bear, What Do You See?, Bill Martin Jr., and Eric Carle																				✓
Building Roads, Judith Bauer Stamper		✓																	
Building Strong Bridges, Kana Riley		✓																	

TITLE and AUTHOR

TITLE and AUTHOR	DESCRIPTION						ORGANIZATION				INFORMATIONAL TEXT STRUCTURE						LITERARY COMPOSING							
	STRONG VERBS	ATTRIBUTE ADJECTIVES	COMPARISONS	PERSONIFICATION	ONOMATOPOEIA	SPECIFICITY	BEGINNINGS	ENDINGS	TIME TRANSITIONS	PLACE TRANSITIONS	MAIN IDEA	MAIN IDEA WITH EXAMPLES	STEP SEQUENCING WITH SUPPORTING DETAILS	COMPARISON	DEFINITION	CAUSE and EFFECT	ALLITERATION	CONTRAST	EMBEDDED DEFINITION	CLUES TO PROVIDE INFERENCE	REPETITION	SENTENCE VARIATION	DIALOGUE TAGS	VOICE
Building Things, Brian and Jillian Cutting	✓							✓																
Bunny Bungalow, Cynthia Rylant							✓												✓					✓
Bunny Cakes, Rosemary Wells				✓																				
Cactus Hotel, Brenda Z. Guiberson									✓					✓										
Canoe Days, Gary Paulsen																								✓
Can't You Sleep, Little Bear?, Martin Waddell																								
Castle, David Macaulay								✓			✓													
Catch the Wind!: All About Kites, Gail Gibbons							✓					✓									✓			
Catfish and Spaghetti, Marcia S. Freeman							✓				✓	✓		✓										
Cecily Cicada, Kita Helmetag Murdock																								
Central Park Serenade, Laura Godwin			✓																					
Charlie Needs a Cloak, Tomie dePaola														✓										
Check It Out!: The Book About Libraries, Gail Gibbons									✓															
Chester's Way, Kevin Henkes							✓																	

Title											
Chicka Chicka Boom Boom, Bill Martin Jr. and John Archambault				✓						✓	
Chicken Soup with Rice: A Book of Months, Maurice Sendak						✓				✓	
Chicken Sunday, Patricia Polacco									✓		
Chimps Don't Wear Glasses, Laura Joffe Numeroff									✓	✓	
Chrysanthemum, Kevin Henkes									✓		
Clap Your Hands, Lorinda Bryan Cauley											✓
Clay Hernandez: A Mexican American, Diane Hoyt-Goldsmith		✓							✓		
Click, Clack, Moo: Cows That Type, Doreen Cronin									✓	✓	
Clifford and the Halloween Parade, Norman Bridwell											
Clifford, We Love You, Norman Bridwell		✓							✓	✓	
Coast to Coast, Marcia S. Freeman					✓						
Cock-a-Doodle Doo!: What Does It Sound Like to You?, Marc Robinson										✓	
Comet's Nine Lives, Jan Brett				✓					✓		
Commotion in the Ocean, Giles Andreae				✓					✓	✓	
Conquering Mount Everest, Jackie Glassman							✓				
Cooking and Change, Paul McEvoy									✓	✓	
Corals, Lynn M. Stone									✓		
Country Crossing, Jim Aylesworth									✓	✓	
Crash! Bang! Boom!, Peter Spier									✓		
Crocodile Tea, Marcia Vaughan		✓							✓	✓	
Crow Boy, Taro Yashima			✓							✓	

TITLE and AUTHOR

TITLE and AUTHOR	DESCRIPTION						ORGANIZATION				INFORMATIONAL TEXT STRUCTURE			LITERARY COMPOSING										
	STRONG VERBS	ATTRIBUTE ADJECTIVES	COMPARISONS	PERSONIFICATION	ONOMATOPOEIA	SPECIFICITY	BEGINNINGS	ENDINGS	TIME TRANSITIONS	PLACE TRANSITIONS	MAIN IDEA	MAIN IDEA WITH EXAMPLES	STEP SEQUENCING WITH SUPPORTING DETAILS	COMPARISON	DEFINITION	CAUSE and EFFECT	ALLITERATION	CONTRAST	EMBEDDED DEFINITION	CLUES TO PROVIDE INFERENCE	REPETITION	SENTENCE VARIATION	DIALOGUE TAGS	VOICE
Crunch Munch, Jonathan London						✓																		
Daisy and the Egg, Jane Simmons								✓																
Dear Grandma, Avelyn Davidson									✓												✓			
Desert Racers, Tracy Nelson Maurer							✓		✓										✓	✓				
Deserts, Gail Gibbons								✓	✓															
Design It! Build It!, Susan Ring																								
Dinosaurs, Dinosaurs, Byron Barton									✓													✓		
Dinosaurs, Melvin Berger														✓										
Dirt, Luana K. Mitten and Mary Wagner								✓	✓															
Do You Know It's Spring?, Allan Fowler																								
Do You Want To Be My Friend?, Eric Carle								✓	✓															
Does a Kangaroo Have a Mother, Too?, Eric Carle																						✓		
Dogs Don't Wear Sneakers, Laura Joffe Numeroff								✓	✓															
Dolphins, Tammy Everts and Bobbie Kalman																	✓				✓			

Title																						
Dominic, William Steig						✓																
Duck, Duck, Goose!: (A Coyote's on the Loose!), Karen Beaumont						✓																
Eaglet's World, Evelyn White Minshull				✓																		
Earrings!, Judith Viorst						✓																
Eating the Alphabet, Lois Elhert											✓											
Encounter, Jane Yolen						✓																
Everything Under the Sun, Marcia S. Freeman						✓	✓		✓	✓						✓						
Exploring Everyday Wonders, Natattlie Lunis and Nancy White						✓																
Farming, Gail Gibbons						✓																
Feeling Things, Allan Fowler		✓		✓		✓							✓									
Fish, Katy Pike and Garda Turner						✓								✓								
Flavors From Plants, Jennifer Blizin Gillis	✓					✓																
Flood, Mary Calhoun			✓																			
Flossie and the Fox, Pat McKissack						✓																
Flower Garden, Eve Bunting		✓																				
Flowers, Paul McEvoy						✓			✓													
Fossils Tell of Long Ago, Aliki						✓													✓			
Friction, Patty Whitehouse			✓																			✓
Froggy Bakes a Cake, Jonathan London				✓																		
Froggy Gets Dressed, Jonathan London		✓																				
Froggy Goes to the Doctor, Jonathan London		✓		✓																		
Froggy Learns to Swim, Jonathan London		✓		✓																		

TITLE and AUTHOR

TITLE and AUTHOR	DESCRIPTION			ORGANIZATION			INFORMATIONAL TEXT STRUCTURE						LITERARY COMPOSING											
	STRONG VERBS	ATTRIBUTE ADJECTIVES	COMPARISONS	PERSONIFICATION	ONOMATOPOEIA	SPECIFICITY	BEGINNINGS	ENDINGS	TIME TRANSITIONS	PLACE TRANSITIONS	MAIN IDEA	MAIN IDEA WITH EXAMPLES	STEP SEQUENCING WITH SUPPORTING DETAILS	COMPARISON	DEFINITION	CAUSE and EFFECT	ALLITERATION	CONTRAST	EMBEDDED DEFINITION	CLUES TO PROVIDE INFERENCE	REPETITION	SENTENCE VARIATION	DIALOGUE TAGS	VOICE
Froggy's Baby Sister, Jonathan London					✓			✓																
Frogs and Toads and Tadpoles, Too!, Allan Fowler								✓	✓						✓					✓	✓			✓
From Farms to You, Paul McEvoy									✓	✓			✓											
From the Factory, Nancy White									✓															
Fungi, Mary Kay Carson								✓	✓						✓	✓								✓
Galimoto, Karen Lynn Williams																								✓
Germs Make Me Sick!, Melvin Berger									✓															✓
Gert & Frieda, Anita Riggio														✓										
Getting Dinner, Jennifer Blizin Gillis			✓					✓	✓			✓			✓	✓		✓	✓	✓	✓			✓
Getting Ready to Race, Susan Ring								✓	✓															
Giants, Wendy Blaxland			✓						✓													✓		
Goblins in Green, Nicholas Heller																		✓		✓				
Going to the City, Marcia S. Freeman									✓						✓									
Going West, Jean Van Leeuwen							✓																✓	

Graph It!, Jennifer Osborne

Growing a Kitchen Garden, Natalie Lunis

Growing Colors, Bruce McMillan

Growing Frogs, Vivian French

Hailstones and Halibut Bones, Mary O'Neill

Happy Birthday, Moon, Frank Asch

Harriet, You'll Drive Me Wild!, Mem Fox

Harry the Dirty Dog, Gene Zion

Have You Seen Trees?, Joanne Oppenheim

Helga's Dowry: A Troll Love Story, Tomie dePaola

Henny Penny, Paul Galdone

Henry and Beezus, Beverly Cleary

Henry Hikes to Fitchburg, D.B. Johnson

Hershel and the Hanukkah Goblins, Eric Kimmel

Hey! Get Off Our Train, John Burningham

Hey, Al, Arthur Yoriuk

How a House is Built, Gail Gibbons

How Do Apples Grow?, Betsy Maestro

How Do You Know It's Spring?, Allan Fowler

How Do You Know It's Winter?, Allan Fowler

How I Became a Pirate, Melinda Long

How I Spent My Summer Vacation, Mark Teague

Hurray for Plants, Jennifer Blizin Gillis

TITLE and AUTHOR

TITLE and AUTHOR	DESCRIPTION						ORGANIZATION				INFORMATIONAL TEXT STRUCTURE						LITERARY COMPOSING							
	STRONG VERBS	ATTRIBUTE ADJECTIVES	COMPARISONS	PERSONIFICATION	ONOMATOPOEIA	SPECIFICITY	BEGINNINGS	ENDINGS	TIME TRANSITIONS	PLACE TRANSITIONS	MAIN IDEA	MAIN IDEA WITH EXAMPLES	STEP SEQUENCING WITH SUPPORTING DETAILS	COMPARISON	DEFINITION	CAUSE and EFFECT	ALLITERATION	CONTRAST	EMBEDDED DEFINITION	CLUES TO PROVIDE INFERENCE	REPETITION	SENTENCE VARIATION	DIALOGUE TAGS	VOICE
Hurricane, David Wiesner								✓																
Hush, Mingfong Ho																						✓		
I Can Be an Author, Ray Broekel					✓																			✓
I Love You the Purplest, Barbara Joosse																				✓				
I Loved You Before You Were Born, Anne Bowen									✓															
I Need a Lunch Box, Jeannette Caines and Pat Cummings									✓													✓		
I Wish I Were a Butterfly, James Howe									✓															
Ida Early Comes Over the Mountain, Robert Burch																					✓			
If You Give a Moose a Muffin, Laura Joffe Numeroff									✓									✓						
If You Give a Mouse a Cookie, Laura Joffe Numeroff									✓									✓						
If You Give a Pig a Pancake, Laura Joffe Numeroff									✓									✓						
If You Take a Mouse to School, Laura Joffe Numeroff																		✓						
In November, Cynthia Rylant						✓												✓					✓	
In the Garden, David M. Schwartz									✓												✓	✓		✓

Title
Incredible Ned, Bill Maynard
Insects, Katy Pike
Inside Mouse, Outside Mouse, Lindsay Barrett George
Inventions, Jennifer Osborne
Invertebrates, Lynn Stone
Investigating Rocks, Natalie Lunis and Nancy White
Is it Alive?, Marcia S. Freeman
Is It Time?, Jane Campbell
Is There Life in Outer Space?, Franklyn M. Branley
Is Your Mama a Llama?, Deborah Guarino
It Could Still Be a Fish, Allan Fowler
It Could Still Be a Rock, Allan Fowler
It Could Still Be a Tree, Allan Fowler
It's a Good Thing There Are Insects, Allan Fowler
It's Best to Leave a Snake Alone, Allan Fowler
It's Spring!, Samantha Berger and Pamela Chanko
It's Winter, Linda Glaser
James and the Giant Peach, Roald Dahl
Johnny Appleseed, Steven Kellogg
Jumanji, Chris Van Allsburg
Just Because I Am a Child, Lauren Murphy Payne
Kakadu Jack, Brenda Parkes
Kate's Giants, Valiska Gregory

TITLE and AUTHOR

TITLE and AUTHOR	DESCRIPTION		ORGANIZATION				INFORMATIONAL TEXT STRUCTURE							LITERARY COMPOSING										
	STRONG VERBS	ATTRIBUTE ADJECTIVES	COMPARISONS	PERSONIFICATION	ONOMATOPOEIA	SPECIFICITY	BEGINNINGS	ENDINGS	TIME TRANSITIONS	PLACE TRANSITIONS	MAIN IDEA	MAIN IDEA WITH EXAMPLES	STEP SEQUENCING WITH SUPPORTING DETAILS	COMPARISON	DEFINITION	CAUSE and EFFECT	ALLITERATION	CONTRAST	EMBEDDED DEFINITION	CLUES TO PROVIDE INFERENCE	REPETITION	SENTENCE VARIATION	DIALOGUE TAGS	VOICE
Kenya's Word, Linda Trice			✓																					
Kindle Me a Riddle: A Pioneer Story, Roberta Karim								✓																
King Bob's New Clothes, Dom DeLuise																					✓	✓		
Kite Sail High, Ruth Heller					✓					✓					✓									
Land of the Dark, Land of the Light: The Arctic National Wildlife Refuge, Karen Pandell														✓						✓		✓		
Last Summer with Maizon, Jacqueline Woodson													✓											✓
Leaf Jumpers, Carole Gerber									✓					✓										
Leaping Frogs, Melvin Berger									✓						✓									
Let's Do It Together, Denise M. Jordan									✓	✓					✓									✓
Let's Experiment, Natalie Lunis and Nancy White												✓												
Let's Go Home: The Wonderful Things About a House, Cynthia Rylant			✓															✓						
Let's Look At Rocks, Luana K. Mitten and Mary Wagner																✓					✓			
Library Lil, Suzanne Williams																								✓

Title												
Life Cycle of a Dog, Angela Royston									✓			
Life Cycle of a Monarch Butterfly, Jennifer Blizin Gillis		✓							✓			
Life in a Tree, Melvin Berger			✓									
Life in America's First Cities, Sally Senzell Isaacs					✓				✓			
Life in the Sea, Melvin Berger			✓								✓	
Light, Melvin Berger	✓											
Like a Windy Day, Frank Asch				✓								
Like Butter on Pancakes, Jonathan London		✓	✓									
Limousines, Tracy Nelson Maurer		✓										
Listen to This, Patty Whitehouse	✓										✓	
Little Cloud, Eric Carle												
Little Green, Keith Baker	✓										✓	
Little House on the Prairie, Laura Ingalls Wilder		✓										
Little Polar Bear and the Husky Pup, Hans de Beer		✓										
Little Quack, Lauren Thompson			✓									
Little Red Riding Hood: A Newfangled Prairie Tale, Lisa Campbell Ernst			✓									
Living Colors, Marcia S. Freeman	✓	✓										
Louie, Ezra Jack Keats		✓										
Mack Made Movies, Don Brown		✓	✓									
Make Mine Ice Cream, Melvin Berger		✓	✓					✓				
Make Way for Ducklings, Robert McCloskey			✓									
Making Mount Rushmore, Anastasia Suen		✓										
Mama Cat Has Three Kittens, Denise Fleming	✓	✓										

TITLE and AUTHOR

TITLE and AUTHOR	DESCRIPTION						ORGANIZATION				INFORMATIONAL TEXT STRUCTURE			LITERARY COMPOSING										
	Strong Verbs	Attribute Adjectives	Comparisons	Personification	Onomatopoeia	Specificity	Beginnings	Endings	Time Transitions	Place Transitions	Main Idea	Main Idea with Examples	Step Sequencing with Supporting Details	Comparison	Definition	Cause and Effect	Alliteration	Contrast	Embedded Definition	Clues to Provide Inference	Repetition	Sentence Variation	Dialogue Tags	Voice
Mammal Moms, Marcia S. Freeman			✓															✓						
Manatee: On Location, Kathy Darling						✓			✓								✓							
Map It!, Elspeth Leacock										✓														
Mapping Penny's World, Loreen Leedy									✓															
Marsh Morning, Marianne Berkes							✓																	
Maurice's Room, Paula Fox								✓																
Mexico City is Muy Grande, Marlene Perez							✓	✓	✓															
Mice Squeak, We Speak, Tomie dePaola							✓																	
Mike Fink, Steven Kellogg			✓			✓																		
Mike Mulligan and His Steam Shovel, Virginia Lee Burton						✓																	✓	
Mirandy and Brother Wind, Pat McKissack				✓																	✓			
Miss Nelson is Back, Harry Allard and James Marshall																								
Miss Nelson is Missing!, Harry Allard and James Marshall								✓																

Title										
Miss Tizzy, Libba Moore Gray	✓									
Moja Means One: Swahili Counting Book, Muriel Feelings					✓					
Mojave, Diane Siebert			✓							
Mommy Go Away!, Lynne Jonell			✓							
Monarch Butterflies, Gail Gibbons				✓						
Monkey Do!, Allan Ahlberg			✓							
Moonbear's Pet, Frank Asch			✓							
More Similes, Joan Hanson		✓								
Morning, Noon, and Night, Jean Craighead George		✓	✓							
Mouse Mess, Linnea Riley			✓							
Mr. Noisy Builds a House, Luella Connelly			✓	✓						
Mr. Willowby's Christmas Tree, Robert Barry				✓						
Mrs. Katz and Tush, Patricia Polacco					✓					
Mrs. Mack, Patricia Polacco		✓								
My Beautiful Child, Lisa Desimini and Matt Mahurin						✓				
My Five Senses, Aliki			✓			✓	✓			
My Great-Aunt Arizona, Gloria Houston			✓	✓						
My Hands, Aliki			✓	✓						
My Mama Says There Aren't Any Zombies, Ghosts, Vampires, Creatures, Demons, Monsters, Fiends, Goblins, or Things, Judith Viorst					✓		✓			
My Visit to the Aquarium, Aliki			✓							
Nana Upstairs & Nana Downstairs, Tomie De Paolo				✓						

TITLE and AUTHOR

Title and Author	DESCRIPTION						ORGANIZATION				INFORMATIONAL TEXT STRUCTURE						LITERARY COMPOSING							
	STRONG VERBS	ATTRIBUTE ADJECTIVES	COMPARISONS	PERSONIFICATION	ONOMATOPOEIA	SPECIFICITY	BEGINNINGS	ENDINGS	TIME TRANSITIONS	PLACE TRANSITIONS	MAIN IDEA	MAIN IDEA WITH EXAMPLES	STEP SEQUENCING WITH SUPPORTING DETAILS	COMPARISON	DEFINITION	CAUSE and EFFECT	ALLITERATION	CONTRAST	EMBEDDED DEFINITION	CLUES TO PROVIDE INFERENCE	REPETITION	SENTENCE VARIATION	DIALOGUE TAGS	VOICE
Nasty, Stinky Sneakers, Eve Bunting										✓													✓	
Needs, Brenda Parkes																								
Night in the Barn, Faye Gibbons				✓		✓												✓				✓		
Nothing Ever Happens on 90th Street, Roni Schotter																								
Now One Foot, Now The Other, Tomie dePaola							✓		✓															
Oceans, Katy Pike and Maureen O'Keefe									✓								✓							
Off We Go!, Jane Yolen			✓							✓								✓						
Old Black Fly, Jim Aylesworth																								
On Monday When It Rained, Cherryl Kachenmeister										✓											✓			
On the Day You Were Born, Debra Fraiser										✓														
One Frog, One Fly, Wendy Blaxland																						✓		
One Hundred Hungry Ants, Elinor J. Pinczes																						✓		
One Small Place by the Sea, Barbara Brenner					✓															✓				
One Spring Day and Night, Patty Whitehouse					✓					✓														✓

Title																
One Stormy Night, Joy Cowley														✓		
Oonawassee Summer, Melissa Forney		✓														✓
Our Attribute Walk, Luana K. Mitten and Mary Wagner																✓
Out of the Ocean, Debra Fraiser,											✓	✓				
Outside and Inside Sharks, Sandra Markle						✓		✓			✓	✓				
Owl Babies, Martin Waddell												✓				
Owl Moon, Jane Yolen											✓	✓	✓			
Ox-Cart Man, Donald Hall											✓	✓				
Paddle-to-the-Sea, Holling Clancy Holling											✓	✓	✓	✓		
Pancakes, Pancakes!, Eric Carle									✓		✓	✓				
Pasta, Please!, Melvin Berger												✓				
Patterns in Nature, Jennifer Blizin Gillis							✓				✓	✓				
Peep!, Kevin Luthardt											✓	✓				
People and the Sea, Sharon Dalgleish and Garda Turner	✓									✓			✓	✓		
People Everywhere, Jeri Cipriano											✓	✓				
People of the Rain Forest, Ted O'Hare												✓				
Perfect Pretzels, Marcie Bovetz	✓		✓	✓							✓	✓				
Peter's Chair, Ezra Jack Keats												✓				
Phoebe's Revolt, Natalie Babbett												✓				
Pickles and Preserves, Judith Bauer Stamper				✓								✓				
Pickles to Pittsburgh, Judi Barrett					✓							✓				
Piggie Pie!, Margie Palatini												✓				
Pigs, Gail Gibbons												✓				

TITLE and AUTHOR

TITLE and AUTHOR	STRONG VERBS	ATTRIBUTE ADJECTIVES	COMPARISONS	PERSONIFICATION	ONOMATOPOEIA	SPECIFICITY	BEGINNINGS	ENDINGS	TIME TRANSITIONS	PLACE TRANSITIONS	MAIN IDEA	MAIN IDEA WITH EXAMPLES	STEP SEQUENCING WITH SUPPORTING DETAILS	COMPARISON	DEFINITION	CAUSE and EFFECT	ALLITERATION	CONTRAST	EMBEDDED DEFINITION	CLUES TO PROVIDE INFERENCE	REPETITION	SENTENCE VARIATION	DIALOGUE TAGS	VOICE
	DESCRIPTION						**ORGANIZATION**		**INFORMATIONAL TEXT STRUCTURE**					**LITERARY COMPOSING**										
Pigsty, Mark Teague								✓																
Planes, Ian Rohr								✓					✓											
Planets, Gail Gibbons								✓	✓															
Polar Bear, Polar Bear, What Do You Hear?, Bill Martin Jr.																						✓		
Polar Bears, Gail Gibbons								✓	✓															
Polar Express, Chris Van Allsburg				✓																				
Polar Regions, Alison Balance								✓	✓	✓						✓			✓	✓				
Popcorn Science, Natalie Lunis and Nancy White									✓	✓				✓										
Postcards From Pluto: A Tour of the Solar System, Loreen Leedy									✓															
Pottery Place, Gail Gibbons							✓				✓	✓		✓						✓				✓
President's Day, Mir Tamim Ansary																								
Properties of Materials, Marcia S. Freeman			✓																					
Puffins Climb, Penguins Rhyme, Bruce McMillan		✓																✓						
Pumpkin Time, Luana K. Mitten and Mary Wagner									✓															

Title																						
Punia and the King of Sharks, Lee Wardlaw		✓																				
Push and Pull, Marcia S. Freeman	✓																			✓		
Putting It Together, Patty Whitehouse																						
Rabbits and Raindrops, Jim Arnosky	✓																					
Raccoons and Ripe Corn, Jim Arnosky	✓			✓																		
Rain Forest At Night, Ted O'Hare				✓																		
Rainbow Fish, Marcus Fister	✓	✓																				
Rainbows All Around Me, Sandra L. Pinkney	✓			✓																		
Recycle!: A Handbook for Kids, Gail Gibbons				✓																		
Reptiles, Lynn M. Stone				✓		✓		✓														
Roaring Rides, Tracy Nelson Maurer													✓									
Rocks and Soil, Natalie Lunis									✓													
Roll of Thunder, Hear My Cry, Mildred Taylor	✓		✓																			
Salt Hands, Jane Aragon				✓																		
Santa Domingo, Marguerite Henry				✓																		
Sarah, Plain and Tall, Patricia MacLachlan	✓			✓																		
Scatterbrain Sam, Ellen Jackson												✓										
Science Tools, J.A. Randolph				✓		✓																
Sea Anemones, Lynn M. Stone			✓			✓						✓										
Sea Life, Katy Pike and Garda Turner			✓		✓	✓																
Seal Pup Grows Up: The Story of a Harbor Seal, Kathleen Weidner Zoehfeld							✓															
Shades of Black, Sandra L. Pinkney	✓			✓																		
Sharing News, Cynthia Rothman																						

TITLE and AUTHOR

TITLE and AUTHOR	DESCRIPTION						ORGANIZATION		INFORMATIONAL TEXT STRUCTURE								LITERARY COMPOSING							
	STRONG VERBS	ATTRIBUTE ADJECTIVES	COMPARISONS	PERSONIFICATION	ONOMATOPOEIA	SPECIFICITY	BEGINNINGS	ENDINGS	TIME TRANSITIONS	PLACE TRANSITIONS	MAIN IDEA	MAIN IDEA WITH EXAMPLES	STEP SEQUENCING WITH SUPPORTING DETAILS	COMPARISON	DEFINITION	CAUSE and EFFECT	ALLITERATION	CONTRAST	EMBEDDED DEFINITION	CLUES TO PROVIDE INFERENCE	REPETITION	SENTENCE VARIATION	DIALOGUE TAGS	VOICE
Sharks, Seymour Simon									✓	✓					✓						✓			
Shiloh, Phyllis Reynolds Naylor									✓															
Shoeless Joe and Black Betsy, Phil Bildner									✓															
Shoes from Grandpa, Mem Fox									✓															
Shoes, Shoes, Shoes, Ann Morris									✓	✓														
Shorebirds, Melissa Stewart																	✓							✓
Short, Tall, Big or Small?, Kari Jenson Gold																✓				✓				
Should There Be Zoos?, Tony Stead with students																								✓
Signals for Safety, Nancy White								✓	✓															
Simple Machines, Melvin Berger													✓											
"Slowly, Slowly, Slowly," said the Sloth, Eric Carle				✓																				
Slugs and Snails, Colin Walker																						✓		
Smart, Clean Pigs, Allan Fowler										✓								✓			✓			
Smoky Night, Eve Bunting									✓	✓														

Title																								
Snakes Are Hunters, Patricia Lauber							✓																	
Snap Likes Gingersnaps, Rachel Gosset							✓																	
Snowballs, Lois Ehlert									✓							✓								
Snowmen at Night, Caralyn Buehner							✓																	
So That's How the Moon Changes Shape!, Allan Fowler							✓							✓	✓									
So You Want to Be President?, Judith St. George							✓		✓			✓		✓	✓									✓
Solid Shapes, Kari Jenson Gold							✓		✓						✓									
Solid, Liquid or Gas?, Fay Robinson							✓							✓		✓								
Song and Dance Man, Karen Ackerman						✓																		
Sorting It All Out, Luana K. Mitten and Mary Wagner							✓				✓			✓										
Sound, Melvin Berger					✓		✓																	
Sounds of the Farm, Kari Jenson Gold					✓		✓																	
Soup, Robert Newton Peck						✓																✓		
Spiders Are Special Animals, Fred and Jeanne Biddulph						✓																		
Spiders, Gail Gibbons											✓													
Spiders, Lisa Trumbauer														✓										
Spinning a Web, Melvin Berger							✓																	
Sponges, Lynn M. Stone							✓																	
Spring, Tanya Thayer						✓																		
Squirrels All Year Long, Melvin Berger						✓		✓																
Stargazers, Gail Gibbons							✓		✓															
Stellaluna, Jannell Cannon						✓																	✓	
Sticky Stuff, Luana K. Mitten and Mary Wagner						✓				✓				✓									✓	

TITLE and AUTHOR

TITLE and AUTHOR	DESCRIPTION					ORGANIZATION		INFORMATIONAL TEXT STRUCTURE						LITERARY COMPOSING										
	STRONG VERBS	ATTRIBUTE ADJECTIVES	COMPARISONS	PERSONIFICATION	ONOMATOPOEIA	SPECIFICITY	BEGINNINGS	ENDINGS	TIME TRANSITIONS	PLACE TRANSITIONS	MAIN IDEA	MAIN IDEA WITH EXAMPLES	STEP SEQUENCING WITH SUPPORTING DETAILS	COMPARISON	DEFINITION	CAUSE and EFFECT	ALLITERATION	CONTRAST	EMBEDDED DEFINITION	CLUES TO PROVIDE INFERENCE	REPETITION	SENTENCE VARIATION	DIALOGUE TAGS	VOICE
Stone Soup, Ann McGovern																						✓		
Stuart Little, E. B. White							✓	✓																
Subway Sonata, Patricia Lakin							✓									✓								
Summer, Katy Pike							✓	✓																
Sun Up, Sun Down, Gail Gibbons					✓			✓		✓					✓					✓				
Sunflower, David M. Schwartz							✓													✓				
Sunken Treasure, Gail Gibbons							✓	✓																
Super-Completely and Totally the Messiest, Judith Viorst										✓						✓				✓		✓		
Sylvester and the Magic Pebble, William Steig				✓			✓		✓	✓	✓	✓												
Tacky the Penguin, Helen Lester					✓						✓													
Tales of a Fourth Grade Nothing, Judy Blume																								
Tar Beach, Faith Ringgold																						✓		✓
Thanksgiving is…, Louise Borden																								
The Amazing Bone, William Steig						✓																		

- *The American Flag*, Lynda Sorensen
- *The Armadillo from Amarillo*, Lynne Cherry
- *The Barbecue*, Jillian Cutting
- *The Biggest Bear*, Lynd Ward
- *The Biggest, Best Snowman*, Margery Cuyler
- *The Carrot Seed*, Ruth Krauss
- *The Christmas Crocodile*, Bonny Becker
- *The Cloud Book*, Tomie dePaola
- *The Cookie-Store Cat*, Cynthia Rylant
- *The Crane's Gift*, Steve and Megumi Biddle
- *The Day Jake Vacuumed*, Simon James
- *The Day Jimmy's Boa Ate the Wash*, Trinka Hakes Nobel
- *The Empty Pot*, Demi
- *The Everglades*, Jean Craighead George
- *The Gardener*, Sarah Stewart
- *The Gift*, Marcia S. Freeman
- *The Gingerbread Baby*, Jan Brett
- *The Gingerbread Man*, Retold by Jim Aylesworth
- *The Giving Tree*, Shel Silverstein
- *The Great Gracie Chase: Stop That Dog!*, Cynthia Rylant
- *The Great Kapok Tree: A Tale of the Amazon Rain Forest*, Lynne Cherry
- *The Grouchy Ladybug*, Eric Carle

TITLE and AUTHOR

TITLE and AUTHOR	DESCRIPTION		ORGANIZATION			INFORMATIONAL TEXT STRUCTURE							LITERARY COMPOSING											
	STRONG VERBS	ATTRIBUTE ADJECTIVES	COMPARISONS	PERSONIFICATION	ONOMATOPOEIA	SPECIFICITY	BEGINNINGS	ENDINGS	TIME TRANSITIONS	PLACE TRANSITIONS	MAIN IDEA	MAIN IDEA WITH EXAMPLES	STEP SEQUENCING WITH SUPPORTING DETAILS	COMPARISON	DEFINITION	CAUSE and EFFECT	ALLITERATION	CONTRAST	EMBEDDED DEFINITION	CLUES TO PROVIDE INFERENCE	REPETITION	SENTENCE VARIATION	DIALOGUE TAGS	VOICE
The Hat, Jan Brett			✓				✓		✓	✓								✓						
The Honey Makers, Gail Gibbons					✓				✓	✓					✓					✓				
The Important Book, Margaret Wise Brown									✓				✓											
The Library, Sarah Stewart									✓				✓									✓		
The Little Engine That Could, Watty Piper						✓	✓	✓	✓										✓			✓		
The Missing Mitten Mystery, Steven Kellogg									✓															
The Mitten, Jan Brett					✓				✓	✓							✓	✓				✓	✓	
The Money Book, Jennifer Osborne									✓	✓														
The Moon Book, Gail Gibbons																								
The Napping House Wakes Up, Audrey Wood								✓											✓			✓		
The Night Before Christmas, Clement Moore																								
The Other Side, Jacqueline Woodson											✓										✓			
The Pumpkin Book, Gail Gibbons										✓					✓									
The Quiltmaker's Gift, Jeff Brumbeau																✓								

TITLE and AUTHOR

TITLE and AUTHOR	DESCRIPTION						ORGANIZATION		INFORMATIONAL TEXT STRUCTURE					LITERARY COMPOSING										
	STRONG VERBS	ATTRIBUTE ADJECTIVES	COMPARISONS	PERSONIFICATION	ONOMATOPOEIA	SPECIFICITY	BEGINNINGS	ENDINGS	TIME TRANSITIONS	PLACE TRANSITIONS	MAIN IDEA	MAIN IDEA WITH EXAMPLES	STEP SEQUENCING WITH SUPPORTING DETAILS	COMPARISON	DEFINITION	CAUSE and EFFECT	ALLITERATION	CONTRAST	EMBEDDED DEFINITION	CLUES TO PROVIDE INFERENCE	REPETITION	SENTENCE VARIATION	DIALOGUE TAGS	VOICE
The Very Clumsy Click Beetle, Eric Carle			✓																					
The Very Hungry Caterpillar, Eric Carle			✓												✓			✓						
The Very Quiet Cricket, Eric Carle			✓															✓						
The Watsons Go to Birmingham—1963, Christopher Paul Curtis																								✓
The Web of Life, Melvin Berger				✓					✓								✓							
The Wednesday Surprise, Eve Bunting				✓						✓														
The Winter Room, Gary Paulsen				✓																				
The Witch Who Was Afraid of Witches, Alice Low									✓													✓		
The Work Book, Marcia S. Freeman									✓	✓								✓			✓			
The World of Ants, Melvin Berger																								
The World of Dinosaurs, Melvin Berger									✓								✓							
The Worrywarts, Pamela Duncan Edwards																								
Three Pebbles and a Song, Eileen Spinelli																✓								
Through Grandpa's Eyes, Patricia MacLachlan																								

Title														
Thunder Cake, Patricia Polacco		✓												
Tico and the Golden Wings, Leo Lionni		✓	✓											✓
Time for Bed, Mem Fox			✓							✓				
Tool Book, Gail Gibbons				✓										
Tops & Bottoms, Janet Stevens		✓	✓							✓				✓
Town Mouse, Country Mouse, Jan Brett	✓				✓			✓						
Train Song, Diana Siebert			✓	✓						✓				
Trains, Ian Rohr		✓		✓	✓	✓				✓				
Trashy Town, Andrea Zimmerman and David Clemesha		✓												
Trouble with Trolls, Jan Brett		✓												
Trucks, Trucks, Trucks, Peter Sis	✓													
Trupp, Jannell Cannon	✓													
Tuesday, David Wiesner												✓		
Tundra, Lynn M. Stone		✓												
Tunnels, Gail Gibbons		✓												
Turtles Take Their Time, Allan Fowler		✓				✓		✓	✓					
Twilight Comes Twice, Ralph Fletcher	✓					✓	✓							
Two Bad Ants, Chris Van Allsburg		✓										✓		
Umbrella, Taro Yashima		✓												
Verdi, Jannell Cannon	✓	✓	✓											
Vote!, Eileen Christelow					✓									
Wackiest White House Pets, Kathryn Gibbs Davis														
Waiting For Sunday, Carol Blackburn		✓												✓

TITLE and AUTHOR

TITLE and AUTHOR	DESCRIPTION						ORGANIZATION				INFORMATIONAL TEXT STRUCTURE			LITERARY COMPOSING										
	STRONG VERBS	ATTRIBUTE ADJECTIVES	COMPARISONS	PERSONIFICATION	ONOMATOPOEIA	SPECIFICITY	BEGINNINGS	ENDINGS	TIME TRANSITIONS	PLACE TRANSITIONS	MAIN IDEA	MAIN IDEA WITH EXAMPLES	STEP SEQUENCING WITH SUPPORTING DETAILS	COMPARISON	DEFINITION	CAUSE and EFFECT	ALLITERATION	CONTRAST	EMBEDDED DEFINITION	CLUES TO PROVIDE INFERENCE	REPETITION	SENTENCE VARIATION	DIALOGUE TAGS	VOICE
Waiting for Wings, Lois Ehlert										✓														
Walter the Baker, Eric Carle									✓									✓						
Wanted…Mud Blossom, Betsy Byars																					✓			
We're Going on a Bear Hunt, Michael Rosen						✓				✓														
Weather, Robyn Supraner					✓				✓															
Wetlands, Marcia S. Freeman					✓								✓							✓				
Whales, Cynthia Rylant								✓										✓		✓				
Whales, Gail Gibbons						✓			✓					✓				✓						
What am I? Music!, Alain Crozon																		✓						
What Charlie Heard, Mordicai Gerstein										✓														
What Daddies Do Best, Laura Joffe Numeroff										✓				✓		✓								
What Do We Pay For?, Marilyn J. Salomon										✓				✓		✓								
What Do You Do When Something Wants to Eat You?, Steve Jenkins									✓															

Title																			
What Happened to the Dinosaurs?, Franklyn M. Branley											✓							✓	
What Happens to a Hamburger?, Paul Showers			✓					✓							✓		✓		
What Hatches?, Don L. Curry					✓														
What is Hot? What Is Not?, Luana K. Mitten and Mary Wagner										✓									
What Is Place Value?, J. E. Osborne					✓		✓						✓			✓		✓	
What Mommies Do Best, Laura Joffe Numeroff					✓		✓					✓							
What Plant is This?, Marcia S. Freeman	✓	✓			✓	✓						✓						✓	
What Was I Scared Of?, Dr. Seuss												✓							
What's Alive?, Lisa Trumbauer														✓				✓	
Wheels, Brian and Jillian Cutting			✓		✓								✓						
When I Was Little: A Four-Year-Old's Memoir of Her Youth, Jamie Lee Curtis			✓		✓									✓				✓	
When I Was Young in the Mountains, Cynthia Rylant	✓				✓					✓								✓	
When the Elephant Walks, Keiko Kasza					✓									✓				✓	
When the Fly Flew In…, Lisa Westberg Peters					✓								✓						
Where Are You Going? To See My Friend!, Eric Carle and Kazuo Iwamura					✓														
Where Do You Live?, Marcia S. Freeman					✓														
Where Does All The Garbage Go?, Melvin Berger																			
Where Is My Continent?, Robin Nelson		✓			✓											✓			
Where Once There Was a Wood, Denise Fleming		✓			✓														
Where the Red Fern Grows, Wilson Rawls	✓																		
Where the Wild Things Are, Maurice Sendak	✓																		

TITLE and AUTHOR

TITLE and AUTHOR	DESCRIPTION			ORGANIZATION			INFORMATIONAL TEXT STRUCTURE							LITERARY COMPOSING											
	STRONG VERBS	ATTRIBUTE ADJECTIVES	COMPARISONS	PERSONIFICATION	ONOMATOPOEIA	SPECIFICITY	BEGINNINGS	ENDINGS	TIME TRANSITIONS	PLACE TRANSITIONS	MAIN IDEA	MAIN IDEA WITH EXAMPLES	STEP SEQUENCING WITH SUPPORTING DETAILS	COMPARISON	DEFINITION	CAUSE and EFFECT	ALLITERATION	CONTRAST	EMBEDDED DEFINITION	CLUES TO PROVIDE INFERENCE	REPETITION	SENTENCE VARIATION	DIALOGUE TAGS	VOICE
White Snow, Bright Snow, Alvin Tresselt				✓																				
Who am I?, Alain Crozon and Aurelie Lanchais				✓														✓						
Who Eats What? Food Chains and Food Webs, Patricia Lauber							✓	✓																✓
Who Hops?, Katie Davis										✓														
Who Says a Dog Goes Bow-Wow?, Hank De Zutter						✓																		
Why Mosquitoes Buzz in People's Ears, Verna Aardema									✓	✓												✓		
Why People Move, Margaret McNamara																								
Why Polar Bears Like Snow...And Flamingos Don't, Nancy White										✓						✓	✓							✓
Wiggle Waggle, Jonathan London						✓																		
Wilfrid Gordon McDonald Partridge, Mem Fox								✓																
William's Doll, Charlotte Zolotow								✓		✓														
Woolly Sheep and Hungry Goats, Allan Fowler				✓														✓		✓	✓			
Yellow with Other Colors, Victoria Parker										✓										✓		✓		

Title															
You Are a Scientist, Marcia S. Freeman	✓	✓			✓	✓			✓				✓	✓	✓
Young Geographers, Marcia S. Freeman				✓				✓			✓				
Yum! Yuck!, Michaela Morgan		✓	✓		✓					✓		✓		✓	
Zelda and Ivy and the Boy Next Door, Laura McGee Kvasnosky															✓

LITERARY COMPOSING

- VOICE
- DIALOGUE TAGS
- SENTENCE VARIATION
- REPETITION
- CLUES TO PROVIDE INFERENCE
- EMBEDDED DEFINITION
- CONTRAST
- ALLITERATION
- CAUSE and EFFECT
- DEFINITION
- COMPARISON

INFORMATIONAL TEXT STRUCTURE

- STEP SEQUENCING WITH SUPPORTING DETAILS
- MAIN IDEA WITH EXAMPLES
- MAIN IDEA
- PLACE TRANSITIONS
- TIME TRANSITIONS
- ENDINGS
- BEGINNINGS

ORGANIZATION

- SPECIFICITY
- ONOMATOPOEIA
- PERSONIFICATION
- COMPARISONS

DESCRIPTION

- ATTRIBUTE ADJECTIVES
- STRONG VERBS

TITLE and AUTHOR

LITERARY COMPOSING

INFORMATIONAL TEXT STRUCTURE

ORGANIZATION

DESCRIPTION

VOICE
DIALOGUE TAGS
SENTENCE VARIATION
REPETITION
CLUES TO PROVIDE INFERENCE
EMBEDDED DEFINITION
CONTRAST
ALLITERATION
CAUSE and EFFECT
DEFINITION
COMPARISON
STEP SEQUENCING WITH SUPPORTING DETAILS
MAIN IDEA WITH EXAMPLES
MAIN IDEA
PLACE TRANSITIONS
TIME TRANSITIONS
ENDINGS
BEGINNINGS
SPECIFICITY
ONOMATOPOEIA
PERSONIFICATION
COMPARISONS
ATTRIBUTE ADJECTIVES
STRONG VERBS

TITLE and AUTHOR